INSTITUTIONS, INSTITUTIONAL CHANGE
AND ECONOMIC PERFORMANCE

THE POLITICAL ECONOMY OF INSTITUTIONS
AND DECISIONS

editors
James Alt, Harvard University
Douglass North, Washington University in St. Louis

INSTITUTIONS, INSTITUTIONAL CHANGE AND ECONOMIC PERFORMANCE

DOUGLASS C. NORTH

CAMBRIDGE
UNIVERSITY PRESS

Published by the Press Syndicate of the University of Cambridge
The Pitt Building, Trumpington Street, Cambridge CB2 1RP
40 West 20th Street, New York, NY 10011-4211, USA
10 Stamford Road, Oakleigh, Melbourne 3166, Australia

© Cambridge University Press 1990

First published 1990
Reprinted 1991 (twice), 1992, 1993 (twice), 1994

Printed in the United States of America

Library of Congress Cataloging in Publication data is available

A catalogue record for this book is available from the British Library

ISBN 0-521-39416-3 hardback
ISBN 0-521-39734-0 paperback

Contents

Series editor's preface

The Cambridge Series in the Political Economy of Institutions and Decisions is built around attempts to answer two central questions: How do institutions evolve in response to individual incentives, strategies, and choices, and how do institutions affect the performance of political and economic systems? The scope of the series is comparative and historical rather than international or specifically American, and the focus is positive rather than normative.

In this challenging theoretical work, Douglass North examines how to explain the vastly different performances of economies over long periods of time. Asking "What combination of institutions best permits capturing the gains from trade?", he offers a broad perspective on how institutions persist and change, superseding his own earlier work on incentives toward efficient institutions. Now his focus is on the interaction of institutions, defined as any constraint humans devise to shape their interactions, and organizations, created to take advantage of the opportunities presented by institutions in shaping the development of economies. The importance of institutions arises from the costliness of measuring what is valuable, protecting rights, and policing and enforcing agreements. Once created, institutions determine the costs of acting in various ways in political and economic contexts. North applies his theories of the interplay between institutional evolution and political and economic organization to a range of historical examples, including the development of management structures, law merchants, insurance, and financial markets. The synthesis he achieves will be equally valuable to students of economics, history, and politics.

Preface

History matters. It matters not just because we can learn from the past, but because the present and the future are connected to the past by the continuity of a society's institutions. Today's and tomorrow's choices are shaped by the past. And the past can only be made intelligible as a story of institutional evolution. Integrating institutions into economic theory and economic history is an essential step in improving that theory and history.

This study provides the outline of a theory of institutions and institutional change. Although it builds on the earlier studies of institutions that have been the focus of my attention for the past twenty years, it delves much more deeply than the earlier studies into the nature of political and economic institutions and how they change. The specification of exactly what institutions are, how they differ from organizations, and how they influence transaction and production costs is the key to much of the analysis.

The central focus is on the problem of human cooperation – specifically the cooperation that permits economies to capture the gains from trade that were the key to Adam Smith's *Wealth of Nations*. The evolution of institutions that create an hospitable environment for cooperative solutions to complex exchange provides for economic growth. Not all human cooperation is socially productive, of course; indeed, this study is concerned as much with explaining the evolution of institutional frameworks that induce economic stagnation and decline as with accounting for the successes.

My primary objective is to construct a way of approaching the issues – a necessary first step in evolving a theory of institutional change. Therefore, much of the book is devoted to developing the analytical framework. The history I include is illustrative, designed to show the promise of the approach, but far from providing for the kind of hypothesis testing that must ultimately be done. Although my primary message is to economists and economic historians, I believe the argument will be equally interesting to other social scientists. With this in mind, I have attempted to keep the economic terminology to a minimum and make the analysis clear to the noneconomist.

So many people have played a role in the development of the ideas presented here that it is difficult to know where to begin in acknowledging them. The first draft of this manuscript was written while I was a fellow at the Center for Advanced Study in the Behavioral Sciences supported by Grant # BNS 8700864 of the National Science Foundation. Gardner Lindzey, Bob Scott, and the staff established a wonderfully hospitable environment for this enterprise. I owe a particular debt to Carol Baxter, who patiently indoctrinated me into enough of the mysteries of the computer to alter fundamentally (for the better) my way of writing. Robert Keohane, Steven Krasner, Mark Machina, and Ken Sokoloff, fellows at the Center that year, all contributed to the development of this study.

I owe special debts to Barry Weingast and John Nye, with whom I have discussed many of the ideas developed herein and who read and commented extensively on several drafts of this study.

While I was writing this manuscript, I was reading drafts of Thrainn Eggertsson's excellent survey of neoinstitutional economics, *Economic Behavior and Institutions* (Cambridge University Press, 1990). His study clarified my thinking on many issues and contributed to shaping the direction of my own work.

Other colleagues at Washington University – Lee Benham, Art Denzau, John Drobak, Gary Miller, and Norman Schofield – all read an earlier draft and offered valuable suggestions. Others who read an earlier draft and provided valuable comments were James Alt, Robert Bates, Robert Ellickson, Stanley Engerman, Philip Hoffman, and Margaret Levi. However, my debts go far beyond those who read the manuscript. I have presented parts of this study at conferences and university colloquia over the past half dozen years and received many valuable suggestions that have shaped my research agenda.

Ruey Hua Liu, and particularly Werner Troesken and Brad Hansen have been diligent and trustworthy research assistants. Annette Milford has labored long and hard over drafts of this manuscript.

Last but certainly not least, Elisabeth Case has translated my inelegant prose into the English language. More than that, she has borne with me through dejection and inspiration as this study has evolved.

Benzonia, Michigan
January 1990

Part I

Institutions

I

An introduction to institutions and institutional change

Institutions are the rules of the game in a society or, more formally, are the humanly devised constraints that shape human interaction. In consequence they structure incentives in human exchange, whether political, social, or economic. Institutional change shapes the way societies evolve through time and hence is the key to understanding historical change.

That institutions affect the performance of economies is hardly controversial. That the differential performance of economies over time is fundamentally influenced by the way institutions evolve is also not controversial. Yet neither current economic theory nor cliometric history shows many signs of appreciating the role of institutions in economic performance because there as yet has been no analytical framework to integrate institutional analysis into economics and economic history. The objective of this book is to provide such an underlying framework. The implications of the analysis suggest a reexamination of much social science theorizing in general and economics in particular, and provide a new understanding of historical change.

In this study I examine the nature of institutions and the consequences of institutions for economic (or societal) performance (Part I). I then outline a theory of institutional change not only to provide a framework for economic (and other) history, but also to explain how the past influences the present and future, the way incremental institutional change affects the choice set at a moment of time, and the nature of path dependence (Part II). The primary objective of the study is to achieve an understanding of the differential performance of economies through time (Part III).

I

Institutions reduce uncertainty by providing a structure to everyday life. They are a guide to human interaction, so that when we wish to greet friends on the street, drive an automobile, buy oranges, borrow money, form a business, bury our dead, or whatever, we know (or can learn easily) how to perform these tasks. We would readily observe that institutions differ if we were to try to make the same transactions in a different country – Bangladesh for example. In the jargon of the economist, institutions define and limit the set of choices of individuals.

Institutions include any form of constraint that human beings devise to shape human interaction. Are institutions formal or informal? They can be either, and I am interested both in formal constraints – such as rules that human beings devise – and in informal constraints – such as conventions and codes of behavior. Institutions may be created, as was the United States Constitution; or they may simply evolve over time, as does the common law. I am interested in both created and evolving institutions, although for purposes of analysis we may want to examine them separately. Many other attributes of institutions also will be explored.

Institutional constraints include both what individuals are prohibited from doing and, sometimes, under what conditions some individuals are permitted to undertake certain activities. As defined here, they therefore are the framework within which human interaction takes place. They are perfectly analogous to the rules of the game in a competitive team sport. That is, they consist of formal written rules as well as typically unwritten codes of conduct that underlie and supplement formal rules, such as not deliberately injuring a key player on the opposing team. And as this analogy would imply, the rules and informal codes are sometimes violated and punishment is enacted. Therefore, an essential part of the functioning of institutions is the costliness of ascertaining violations and the severity of punishment.

Continuing the sports analogy, taken together, the formal and informal rules and the type and effectiveness of enforcement shape the whole character of the game. Some teams are successful as a consequence of (and have therefore the reputation for) constantly violating rules and thereby intimidating the opposing team. Whether that strategy pays off obviously depends on the effectiveness of monitoring and the severity of punishment. Sometimes codes of conduct – good sportsmanship – constrain players, even though they could get away with successful violations.

A crucial distinction in this study is made between institutions and organizations. Like institutions, organizations provide a structure to human interaction. Indeed when we examine the costs that arise as a consequence of the institutional framework we see they are a result not only of that framework, but also of the organizations that have developed in consequence of that framework. Conceptually, what must be clearly differentiated are the rules from the players. The purpose of the rules is to define the way the game is played. But the objective of the team within that set of rules is to win the game – by a combination of skills, strategy, and coordination; by fair means and sometimes by foul means. Modeling the strategies and the skills of the team as it develops is a separate process from modeling the creation, evolution, and consequences of the rules.

Organizations include political bodies (political parties, the Senate, a city council, a regulatory agency), economic bodies (firms, trade unions, family farms, cooperatives), social bodies (churches, clubs, athletic associations), and educational bodies (schools, universities, vocational training centers). They are groups of individuals bound by some common purpose to achieve objectives. Modeling organizations is analyzing governance structures, skills, and how learning by doing will determine the organization's success over time. Both what organizations come into existence and how they evolve are fundamentally influenced by the institutional framework. In turn they influence how the institutional framework evolves. But as noted above, the emphasis in this study is on the institutions that are the underlying rules of the game and the focus on organizations (and their entrepreneurs) is primarily on their role as agents of institutional change; therefore the emphasis is on the interaction between institutions and organizations. Organizations are created with purposive intent in consequence of the opportunity set resulting from the existing set of constraints (institutional ones as well as the traditional ones of economic theory) and in the course of attempts to accomplish their objectives are a major agent of institutional change.

Separating the analysis of the underlying rules from the strategy of the players is a necessary prerequisite to building a theory of institutions. Defining institutions as the constraints that human beings impose on themselves makes the definition complementary to the choice theoretic approach of neoclassical economic theory. Building a theory of institutions on the foundation of individual choices is a step toward reconciling differences between economics and the other social sciences. The choice theoretic approach is essential because a logically consistent, potentially testable set of hypotheses must be built on a theory of human behavior. The strength of microeconomic theory is that it is constructed on the basis of assumptions about individual human behavior (even though I shall argue for a change in those assumptions in Chapter 3). Institutions are a creation of human beings. They evolve and are altered by human beings; hence our theory must begin with the individual. At the same time, the constraints that institutions impose on individual choices are pervasive. Integrating individual choices with the constraints institutions impose on choice sets is a major step toward unifying social science research.

Institutions affect the performance of the economy by their effect on the costs of exchange and production. Together with the technology employed, they determine the transaction and transformation (production) costs that make up total costs. The initial objective of this study (Part I) is to explain the existence and nature of institutions to specify the way they enter into the cost functions in an economy.

II

The major role of institutions in a society is to reduce uncertainty by establishing a stable (but not necessarily efficient) structure to human interaction. But the stability of institutions in no way gainsays the fact that they are changing. From conventions, codes of conduct, and norms of behavior to statute law, and common law, and contracts between individuals, institutions are evolving and, therefore, are continually altering the choices available to us. The changes at the margin may be so slow and glacial in character that we have to stand back as historians to perceive them, although we live in a world where the rapidity of institutional change is very apparent.

Institutional change is a complicated process because the changes at the margin can be a consequence of changes in rules, in informal constraints, and in kinds and effectiveness of enforcement. Moreover, institutions typically change incrementally rather than in discontinuous fashion. How and why they change incrementally and why even discontinuous changes (such as revolution and conquest) are never completely discontinuous are a result of the imbeddedness of informal constraints in societies. Although formal rules may change overnight as the result of political or judicial decisions, informal constraints embodied in customs, traditions, and codes of conduct are much more impervious to deliberate policies. These cultural constraints not only connect the past with the present and future, but provide us with a key to explaining the path of historical change.

The central puzzle of human history is to account for the widely divergent paths of historical change. How have societies diverged? What accounts for their widely disparate performance characteristics? After all, we all descended from primitive hunting and gathering bands. This divergence is even more perplexing in terms of standard neoclassical and international trade theory, which implies that over time economies, as they traded goods, services, and productive factors, would gradually converge. Although we do observe some convergence among leading industrial nations that trade with each other, an overwhelming feature of the last ten millennia is that we have evolved into radically different religious, ethnic, cultural, political, and economic societies, and the gap between rich and poor nations, between developed and undeveloped nations, is as wide today as it ever was and perhaps a great deal wider than ever before. What explains the divergence? And perhaps equally important, what conditions either lead to further divergences or produce convergence?

There is more to this puzzle. What accounts for societies experiencing long-run stagnation or an absolute decline in economic well-being? The evolutionary hypothesis advanced by Alchian in 1950 would suggest that ubiquitous competition would weed out inferior institutions and reward by survival those that better solve human problems.

Let me briefly retrace my steps in dealing with this central issue. In North and Thomas (1973) we made institutions the determinant of economic performance and relative price changes the source of institutional change. But we had an essentially efficient explanation; changes in relative prices create incentives to construct more efficient institutions. The persistence of inefficient institutions, illustrated by the case of Spain, was a result of fiscal needs of rulers that led to shortened time horizons and therefore a disparity between private incentives and social welfare. Such an anomaly did not fit into the theoretical framework.

In *Structure and Change in Economic History* (North, 1981) I abandoned the efficiency view of institutions. Rulers devised property rights in their own interests and transaction costs resulted in typically inefficient property rights prevailing. As a result it was possible to account for the widespread existence of property rights throughout history and in the present that did not produce economic growth. In that study I raised the question posed by Alchian's evolutionary argument, but had no answer. It was possible to explain the existence of inefficient institutions, but why wouldn't competitive pressures lead to their elimination? Wouldn't the political entrepreneurs in stagnant economies quickly emulate the policies of more successful ones? How can we explain the radically differential performance of economies over long periods of time?

This study answers these questions. The answer hinges on the difference between institutions and organizations and the interaction between them that shapes the direction of institutional change. Institutions, together with the standard constraints of economic theory, determine the opportunities in a society. Organizations are created to take advantage of those opportunities, and, as the organizations evolve, they alter the institutions. The resultant path of institutional change is shaped by (1) the lock-in that comes from the symbiotic relationship between institutions and the organizations that have evolved as a consequence of the incentive structure provided by those institutions and (2) the feedback process by which human beings perceive and react to changes in the opportunity set.

The increasing returns characteristics of an institutional matrix that produces lock-in come from the dependence of the resultant organizations on that institutional framework and the consequent network exter-

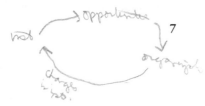

7

nalities that arise. Both the formal and the informal institutional constraints result in particular exchange organizations that have come into existence because of the incentives embodied in the framework and therefore depend on it for the profitability of the activities that they undertake.

Incremental change comes from the perceptions of the entrepreneurs in political and economic organizations that they could do better by altering the existing institutional framework at some margin. But the perceptions crucially depend on both the information that the entrepreneurs receive and the way they process that information. If political and economic markets were efficient (i.e., there were zero transaction costs) then the choices made would always be efficient. That is the actors would always possess true models or if they initially possessed incorrect models the information feedback would correct them. But that version of the rational actor model has simply led us astray. The actors frequently must act on incomplete information and process the information that they do receive through mental constructs that can result in persistently inefficient paths. Transaction costs in political and economic markets make for inefficient property rights, but the imperfect subjective models of the players as they attempt to understand the complexities of the problems they confront can lead to the persistence of such property rights.

We can expand on this characterization of institutional change by contrasting a successful path with one of persistent failure. The first is a familiar story in U.S. economic history – the growth of the economy in the nineteenth century. The basic institutional framework that had evolved by the beginning of that century (the Constitution and the Northwest Ordinance, as well as norms of behavior rewarding hard work) broadly induced the development of economic and political organizations (Congress, local political bodies, family farms, merchant houses, and shipping firms), whose maximizing activities resulted in increased productivity and economic growth both directly and indirectly by an induced demand for educational investment. The educational investment resulted not only in the free public educational system, but in agricultural experiment stations to improve agricultural productivity; the Morrill Act created the land grant public universities.

As economic organizations evolved to take advantage of these opportunities, they not only became more efficient (see Chandler, 1977), but also gradually altered the institutional framework. Not only was the political and judicial framework altered (the Fourteenth Amendment, *Munn* v. *Illinois*) and the structure of property rights modified (the Sherman Act) by the end of the nineteenth century, but so too were many norms of behavior and other informal constraints (reflected in changing attitudes – and norms of behavior – toward slavery, the role of women, and temperance, for example). Both the political and the economic transaction costs and the subjective perceptions of the actors resulted in choices that were certainly not always optimal or unidirectional toward increased productivity or improved economic welfare (however defined). The profitable opportunities were sometimes from tariff creation, the exploitation of slaves, or the formation of a trust. Sometimes, indeed frequently, policies had unintended consequences. In consequence institutions were – and are – always a mixed bag of those that induce productivity increase and those that reduce productivity. Institutional change, likewise, almost always creates opportunities for both types of activity. But on balance nineteenth-century U.S. economic history is a story of economic growth because the underlying institutional framework persistently reinforced incentives for organizations to engage in productive activity however admixed with some adverse consequences.

Now if I describe an institutional framework with a reverse set of incentives to those described in the above paragraph, I will approximate the conditions in many Third World countries today as well as those that have characterized much of the world's economic history. The opportunities for political and economic entrepreneurs are still a mixed bag, but they overwhelmingly favor activities that promote redistributive rather than productive activity, that create monopolies rather than competitive conditions, and that restrict opportunities rather than expand them. They seldom induce investment in education that increases productivity. The organizations that develop in this institutional framework will become more efficient – but more efficient at making the society even more unproductive and the basic institutional structure even less conducive to productive activity. Such a path can persist because the transaction costs of the political and economic markets of those economies together with the subjective models of the actors do not lead them to move incrementally toward more efficient outcomes.

This study sheds light on these contrasting stories by providing a theoretical foundation to the study of institutional change. The next chapter explores the theoretical foundations of the underlying role of institutions – the problem of human cooperation. Then come two key chapters that provide the basic building blocks of a theory of institutions. In Chapter 3 I explore, critically, the behavioral assumptions we employ and suggest modifications in those behavioral assumptions, and in Chapter 4 I provide a theoretical foundation to the costliness of exchange and its surprisingly important but unappreciated implications.

In the next three chapters I successively describe three dimensions of institutions: formal rules and informal constraints, and the effectiveness of their enforcement. Then I am in the position in Chapter 8 to tie together the threads and illustrate the relationship between institutions and transaction and transformation (production) costs.

Institutions

Part II provides a framework to analyze institutional change. Chapter 9 explores organizations and the way they interact with institutions. Chapter 10 deals with the stability characteristics of institutions, which are essential to understanding the nature of institutional change. The change we observe is seldom discontinuous (although I shall explore revolutionary change) but instead is incremental, and the nature of the incremental institutional change together with the imperfect way by which the actors interpret their environment and make choices accounts for path dependency and makes history relevant (Chapter 11).

Part III relates institutions and the way they change to economic performance. In Chapter 12 I consider the theoretical implications of institutional analysis for the performance of economies both at a moment of time and over time. Chapters 13 and 14 apply the analytical framework to economic history. Chapter 13 explores the characteristics of institutional change of successively more complex economies in history and contrasts the stable forms of historical exchange with the dynamic institutional change of Western Europe that led to modern economic growth. The final chapter suggests the implications of systematically integrating institutional analysis into economic history and presents some extended historical applications.

2

Cooperation: the theoretical problem

There is a persistent tension in the social sciences between the theories we construct and the evidence we compile about human interaction in the world around us. It is most striking in economics, where the contrast between the logical implications of neoclassical theory and the performance of economies (however defined and measured) is startling. Certainly neoclassical theory has been a major contribution to knowledge and works well in the analysis of markets in developed countries. At the other end of the scale, however, it does not provide much insight into such organizations as the medieval manor, the Champagne fairs, or the suq (the bazaar market that characterizes much of the Middle East and North Africa). Not only does it not characterize these organizations' exchange process very well, it does not explain the persistence for millennia of what appear to be inefficient forms of exchange.

The disparity in the performance of economies and the persistence of disparate economies through time have not been satisfactorily explained by development economists, despite forty years of immense effort. The simple fact is that the theory employed is not up to the task. The theory is based on the fundamental assumption of scarcity and hence competition; its harmonious implications come from its assumptions about a frictionless exchange process in which property rights are perfectly and costlessly specified and information is likewise costless to acquire. Although the scarcity and hence competition assumption has been robust and has provided the key underpinnings of neoclassical theory, the other assumptions have not survived nearly so well.

For the past thirty years, other economists and other social scientists have been attempting to modify and refine the issues to see just what has been missing from the explanation. Put simply, what has been missing is an understanding of the nature of human coordination and cooperation. Now, that certainly should not surprise a disciple of Adam Smith. Smith was concerned not only with those forms of cooperation that produced collusive and monopolistic outcomes, but also with those forms of cooperation that would permit realization of the gains from trade. However, the confusion and misunderstanding that followed on the heels of Ronald Coase's famous "The Problem of Social Cost" (1960) makes clear how difficult it is for economists to come to terms with the role of institutions in capturing the potential gains from trade. Coase said a number of fundamentally important things in both this essay and his "The Nature of the Firm" (1937). The most important message, one with profound implications for restructuring economic theory, is that when it is costly to transact, institutions matter. And as Wallis and North (1986) have demonstrated in their measurement of the transaction costs going through the market (the transaction sector) in the U.S. economy, it is costly to transact.

I

If economists have been slow to integrate institutions into their theoretical models, they, along with other social scientists, have been quick to explore the problems of cooperation in a game theoretic framework. To apply this approach briefly and in an oversimplified fashion, wealth-maximizing individuals will usually find it worthwhile to cooperate with other players when the play is repeated, when they possess complete information about the other players' past performances, and when there are small numbers of players. Such a crude summary disguises the richness (and ingenuity) of the results of an army of game theorists who have extended, elaborated, and modified (as well as found exceptions to) each of those qualifications to squeeze a great deal more out of them. In subsequent chapters I shall have more to say about game theory, because it provides an excellent foil (very much like the pure neoclassical economic model) against which to compare actual performance.

Let me turn the game upside down. Cooperation is difficult to sustain when the game is not repeated (or there is an end game), when information on the other players is lacking, and when there are large numbers of players. These polar extremes in fact reflect real life contrasts. We usually observe cooperative behavior when individuals repeatedly interact, when they have a great deal of information about each other, and when small numbers characterize the group. But at the other extreme, realizing the economic potential of the gains from trade in a high technology world of enormous specialization and division of labor characterized by impersonal exchange is extremely rare, because one does not necessarily have repeated dealings, nor know the other party, nor deal with a small number of other people. In fact, the essence of impersonal exchange is the antithesis of the condition for game theoretic cooperation. But the modern Western world does in fact exist. How come? A neat, definitive answer to why, both throughout history and in most of the present world economies, the potential gains from trade have not been realized, as well as to why the modern Western world has realized (at least partially) this economic potential, would not only solve the issues of economic development but point toward resolving the larger issues of human conflict that continue to hang over our heads.

The noncoincidence of wealth-maximizing behavior and socially cooperative outcomes has been a key factor in the way game theory has evolved. The so-called prisoner's dilemma that has been a mainstay of game theory is closely allied to Mancur Olson's (1965) free-rider dilemma. Both suggest a discouraging perspective on the problems of human cooperation and coordination. However, the most dismal aspects of Olson's analysis and prisoner dilemma problems reflect the static nature of the analysis and the fact that it is a one-shot game. That is, when the prisoner's dilemma game is played only once, it is a dominant strategy for players to defect and therefore not to achieve what would be an efficient outcome with respect to the aggregate well-being of the players. However, it is well known that defection is not necessarily the dominant strategy if the situation is repeated over and over again, as many collective action problems are. In an iterated prisoner's dilemma game, one that is repeated, there is no dominant strategy. In a now-famous tournament, Robert Axelrod found that the winning strategy under these conditions of continuous repeated play is a strategy of tit-for-tat, one in which a player responds in kind to the action of the other player. This led to Axelrod's celebrated *The Evolution of Cooperation* (1984), an optimistic book about the ability of human beings to devise cooperative solutions to problems without the intervention of a coercive state.

The conditions under which cooperation can be sustained have produced an immense literature, both in game theory and by nongame theorists who are interested in the political-modeling process. Three works that focus on the issues and problems of the maintenance of cooperation will, I believe, highlight the issues we are concerned with in this study.

Russell Hardin (1982) focuses on the *n*-person prisoner's dilemma (PD) and explores the difficulties of collective action in large groups. Hardin emphasizes that the difficulties of collective action depend not just on the size of the group, but also on the ratio of costs to benefits.[1] Conventions (which lead to some form of social order) may arise, particularly when there are asymmetries through which the participants may explore each other's motivations and capabilities in iterated games. Hardin argues that

[1]In a recent historical study of the formation of property rights in natural resource industries in the United States, Libecap (1989) comes to a similar conclusion with respect to the critical role of the ratio of benefits to costs as a determinant of success in efficient property rights formation.

conventions may also come into existence when the participants adopt conditional strategies. However, the conditional strategies involve policing and enforcement (by threats).

Michael Taylor (1982, 1987) explores the conditions under which social order can be maintained in anarchy, that is, without the state. He asserts that community is essential for anarchic social order and that the key features of community are shared common beliefs or norms, direct and complex relationships between members, and reciprocity. Taylor argues that the state destroys the very elements of community (an argument that has been made by Titmuss and others) and indeed, to the degree that altruism plays a role, it too can be minimized or destroyed by the coercive action of the state.

Howard Margolis (1982) develops a model in which individual behavior is in part determined by altruistic motives. Margolis argues that individuals have two types of utility functions, those that favor group-oriented preferences and those that favor selfish preferences, and that individuals make trade-offs between the two. His model allows him to explain certain patterns of voting behavior that do not appear to make sense in the behavioral context of a wealth-maximizing individual.

These three works represent major efforts to examine the conditions by which cooperation can be maintained. It is important at this point to confront an issue that will be a focus of this study: that is, under what conditions can voluntary cooperation exist without the Hobbesian solution of the imposition of a coercive state to create cooperative solutions? Historically the growth of economies has occurred within the institutional framework of well-developed coercive polities. We do not observe political anarchy in high-income countries. On the other hand the coercive power of the state has been employed throughout most of history in ways that have been inimicable to economic growth (North, 1981, Chapter 3). But it is difficult to sustain complex exchange without a third party to enforce agreements. Surely, the jury is still out on what continues to be the fundamental issue for the solution of problems of humankind. Perhaps the most pessimistic perspective is that the arguments of Michael Taylor on community and cooperative solutions do not appear to be viable with large numbers and incomplete information. Norman Schofield, in a perceptive review article on these three works, describes the problem as follows:

The fundamental theoretical problem underlying the question of cooperation is the manner by which individuals attain knowledge of each others preferences and likely behavior. Moreover, the problem is one of common knowledge, since each individual, i, is required not only to have information about others preferences, but also to know that the others have knowledge about i's own preferences and strategies.

Cooperation: the theoretical problem

In the restricted N-person PD, it might be possible to argue that this problem is partially resolvable, in the sense that certain types of actors might have good reason to believe that others are of a particular type. In the restricted context of a community, Taylor's argument makes good sense: social norms will be well understood and will provide the basis for common knowledge and this knowledge will be maintained by mechanisms designed to make acts intelligible. In more general social situations, however, individuals will be less able to make reasonable guesses about other individuals' beliefs. The theoretical problems underlying cooperation can be stated thus: what is the minimal amount that one agent must know in a given milieu about the beliefs and wants of other agents to be able to form coherent notions about their behavior and for this knowledge to be communicable to the others? It seems to me that this problem is the heart of any analysis of community, convention, and cooperation. (Schofield, 1985, pp. 12–13)

II

Game theory highlights the problems of cooperation and explores specific strategies that alter the payoffs to the players. But there is a vast gap between the relatively clean, precise, and simple world of game theory and the complex, imprecise, and fumbling way by which human beings have gone about structuring human interaction. Moreover, game theoretic models, like neoclassical models, assume wealth-maximizing players. But as some of the experimental economics literature demonstrates, human behavior is clearly more complicated than can be encompassed in such a simple behavioral assumption. Although game theory demonstrates the gains from cooperating and defecting in various contexts, it does not provide us with a theory of the underlying costs of transacting and how those costs are altered by different institutional structures. It is necessary to return to the Coase theorem to sort out those issues.

Coase began his essay (1960) by arguing that when it is costless to transact, the efficient competitive solution of neoclassical economics obtains. It does so because the competitive structure of efficient markets leads the parties to arrive costlessly at the solution that maximizes aggregate income regardless of the initial institutional arrangements. The arrangements can be circumvented or even changed in a setting of costless transacting. Now to the extent that these conditions are mimicked in the real world, it is because competition is strong enough via arbitrage and efficient information feedback to approximate the Coase zero transaction cost conditions and the parties can realize the gains from trade inherent in the neoclassical argument. That is, competition eliminates the incomplete and asymmetric information that rewards defection in the game theory models.

But the informational and institutional requirements necessary to achieve these results are stringent. They entail that the players not only have objectives, but choose the correct way to achieve them. But how do the players know the correct way (that is, have the correct theory that will allow them) to achieve their objectives? The neoclassical answer, embodied in substantive (or instrumental) rationality models, is that even though the actors may initially have diverse and erroneous models, the informational feedback process (and arbitraging actors) will correct initially incorrect models, punish deviant behavior, and lead surviving players to the correct models.

An even more stringent implicit requirement of the discipline-of-the-competitive-market model is that when there are significant transaction costs, the consequent institutions of the market will be designed to induce the actors to acquire the essential information that will lead them to the correct models. The implication is not only that institutions are designed to achieve efficient outcomes, but that they can be ignored in economic analysis because they play no independent role in economic performance.

None of these stringent requirements can survive critical scrutiny. Individuals act on incomplete information and with subjectively derived models that are frequently *erroneous;* the information feedback is typically insufficient to correct these subjective models. Institutions are not necessarily or even usually created to be socially efficient; rather they, or at least the formal rules, are created to serve the interests of those with the bargaining power to devise new rules. In a zero-transaction-cost world, bargaining strength does not affect the efficiency of outcomes, but in a world of positive transaction costs it does and given the *lumpy* indivisibilities that characterize institutions, it shapes the direction of long-run economic change.

If economies realize the gains from trade by creating relatively efficient institutions, it is because under certain circumstances the private objectives of those with the bargaining strength to alter institutions produce institutional solutions that turn out to be or evolve into socially efficient ones. The subjective models of the actors, the effectiveness of the institutions at reducing transaction costs, and the degree to which the institutions are *malleable* and respond to changing preferences and relative prices determine those circumstances. Therefore, we next explore the underlying determinants of human behavior, the costs of transacting, and the makeup of institutions.

3

The behavioral assumptions in a theory of institutions

All theorizing in the social sciences builds, implicitly or explicitly, upon conceptions of human behavior. Some of the approaches rest on the expected-utility assumption in economic theory or the extension of that behavioral assumption into other social science disciplines, loosely termed rational choice theory. Other approaches raise some quite fundamental questions about the traditional economic approach. Although I know of very few economists who really believe that the behavioral assumptions of economics accurately reflect human behavior, they do (mostly) believe that such assumptions are useful for building models of market behavior in economics and, though less useful, are still the best game in town for studying politics and the other social sciences.

I believe that these traditional behavioral assumptions have prevented economists from coming to grips with some very fundamental issues and that a modification of these assumptions is essential to further progress in the social sciences. The motivation of the actors is more complicated (and their preferences less stable) than assumed in received theory. More controversial (and less understood) among the behavioral assumptions, usually, is the implicit one that the actors possess cognitive systems that provide *true* models of the worlds about which they make choices or, at the very least, that the actors receive information that leads to convergence of divergent initial models. This is patently wrong for most of the interesting problems with which we are concerned. Individuals make choices based on subjectively derived models that diverge among individuals and the information the actors receive is so incomplete that in most cases these divergent subjective models show no tendency to converge. Only when we understand these modifications in the behavior of the actors can we make sense out of the existence and structure of institutions and explain the direction of institutional change. In this chapter I first examine expected utility theory, then explore issues of motivation and the relationship between the complexity of the environment and the

17

subjective models of reality that the actors possess, and finally tie in these observations to explain the existence of institutions.

I

What behavior then is consistent with an institution-free world (or at least one where the institutions function costlessly)? I begin by quoting Mark Machina's characterization of what is meant by expected utility theory, which is the underlying behavioral assumption of neoclassical economics:

As a theory of individual behavior, the expected utility model shares many of the underlying assumptions of standard consumer theory. In each case we assume that the objects of choice, either commodity bundles or lotteries, can be unambiguously and objectively described, and that situations which ultimately imply the same set of availabilities (e.g., the same budget set) will lead to the same choice. In each case we also assume that the individual is able to perform the mathematical operations necessary to actually determine the set of availabilities, e.g, to add up the quantities in different size containers or calculate the probabilities of compound or conditional events. Finally, in each case we assume that preferences are transitive, so that if an individual prefers one object (either a commodity bundle or a risky prospect) to a second, and prefers this second object to a third, he or she will prefer the first object to the third. (Machina, 1987, pp. 124–5)

In the past twenty years, this approach has come under severe attack and also has found strong defenders. The severe attack has come from experimental economic methods, research by psychologists, and other empirical work, all of which have revealed major empirical anomalies associated with this approach.[1] Briefly, these fall into the following categories: violations of the transitivity assumptions; framing effects, where alternative means of representing the same choice problem can yield different choices; preference reversals, where the ordering of objects on the basis of their reported valuations contradicts the ordering implied in direct choice situations; and problems in the formulation, manipulation, and processing of subjective probabilities in uncertain choices.

Most of these anomalies have emerged in the context of carefully de-

---

[1]The extensive literature dealing with these issues is best seen in the proceedings of a conference held at the University of Chicago in October 1985 entitled *The Behavioral Foundations of Economic Theory* (Hogarth and Reder, eds.). At this conference a large number of psychologists, economists, and a few members of other social science disciplines gathered and explored fruitfully the complexities and issues involved in the behavioral analysis employed by economists. In addition, see the survey by Mark Machina in the first issue of the *Journal of Economic Perspectives* (1987), the 1987 Annual Lecture to the Scottish Economic Society given by Frank Hahn (Hahn, 1987), and *Rationality in Economics* by Shaun Hargreaves-Heap (1989).

signed experiments, which deal with rather limited sets of issues. As I shall be at pains to discuss later in this chapter, they do not appear directly applicable to the immediate subject here, which is the role of behavioral assumptions in the formation and indeed in the existence of institutions. But they do form the basis for thinking critically about the set of issues we must examine.

Perhaps the best summary of the neoclassical behavioral assumptions was made by Sidney Winter. He argues that there are seven steps to what he calls the classic defense of neoclassical behavioral assumptions. They are:

1. The economic world is reasonably viewed as being in equilibrium.
2. Individual economic actors repeatedly face the same choice situations or a sequence of very similar choices.
3. The actors have stable preferences and thus evaluate the outcomes of individual choices according to stable criteria.
4. Given repeated exposure, any individual actor could identify and would seize any available opportunity for improving outcomes and, in the case of business firms, would do so on the pain of being eliminated by competition.
5. Hence no equilibrium can arise in which individual actors fail to maximize their preferences.
6. Because the world is in approximate equilibrium, it exhibits at least approximately the patterns employed by the assumptions that the actors are maximizing.
7. The details of the adaptive process are complex and probably actor and situation specific. By contrast, the regularities associated with optimization equilibrium are comparatively simple; considerations of parsimony, therefore, dictate that the way to progress in economic understanding is to explore these regularities theoretically and to compare the results with other observations.[2]

It is important to emphasize a particular point here. The behavioral assumptions that economists use do not imply that everybody's behavior is consistent with rational choice. But they do rest fundamentally on the assumption that competitive forces will see that those who behave in a rational manner, as described above, will survive, and those who do not will fail; and that therefore in an evolutionary, competitive situation (one that employs the basic assumption of all neoclassical economics of scarcity and competition), the behavior that will be continuously observed will be that of people who have acted according to such standards. Before I criticize this argument and its extension to institutional economic theo-

[2]Winter in Hogarth and Reder (1986), p. S-429.

ry, it is important to note very carefully its successes. In those instances where something approximating the conditions described above exist, the neoclassical model has been a very effective model for analyzing economic phenomena. For example, in the study of finance, where financial markets tend to have many of the characteristics described above, substantial successes have been made using the straightforward assumptions just described.[3]

II

To explore the deficiencies of the rational choice approach as it relates to institutions, we must delve into two particular aspects of human behavior: (1) motivation and (2) deciphering the environment. Human behavior appears to be more complex than that embodied in the individual utility function of economists' models. Many cases are ones not simply of wealth-maximizing behavior, but of altruism and of self-imposed constraints, which radically change the outcomes with respect to the choices that people actually make. Similarly, we find that people decipher the environment by processing information through preexisting mental constructs through which they understand the environment and solve the problems they confront. Both the computational abilities of the players and the complexity of the problems to be solved must be taken into account in understanding the issues. We explore first the motivation of the actors.

In recent years the work of sociobiologists and economists has been combined to explore the many parallels between the underlying features of genetic survival and evolutionary development among animals and similar patterns of behavior among human beings. Many economists have found that this approach is not only congenial, but that it also reveals a great deal about human behavior. Jack Hirshleifer (1987) compares biological evolutionary models with socioeconomic ones as follows:

Evolutionary models share certain properties. First of all, they concern populations. Even where we seem to be speaking of single entities, if the course of change is evolutionary it can be described in terms of changing populations of micro-units. Thus, the evolutionary course of a disease within a single human body is a function of the relations among populations of bacteria, antibodies, cells, and so on. Or the evolution of a single nation's economy is the result of changing relations among populations of individuals, trading units, and the like. Evolutionary models represent a combination of constancy (inheritance) and variation. There must be an unchanging as well as a changing element, and even the changing

---

[3]The essays by Charles Plott and Robert Lucas in Hogarth and Reder (1986) provide a thoughtful defense of the assumptions of the neoclassical model in specific contexts.

element itself must be heritable if a system can be said to evolve. In biological evolution, the emphasis is upon differential survival and reproduction of organismic types or characters from one generation to the next. Here the constancy is due to Mendelian inheritance of permanent patterns of coded genetic instructions (genes). Variation stems from a number of forces, including internal mutations of these instructions (genetic copying errors), recombination of genes in sexual reproduction, and the external pressure of natural selection. Socioeconomic evolution mainly concerns the differential growth and survival of patterns of social organization. The main inheritance element is the deadweight of social inertia, supported by intentionally taught tradition. As for variation, there are analogues to mutations (copying errors as we learn traditions). Also, natural selection is still effective. Finally, *imitation* and *rational* thought constitute additional non-genetic sources of socioeconomic variation. (Hirshleifer, 1987, p. 221)

Efficiency in this evolutionary model does not necessarily have the nice properties that economists give the term, but frequently is associated with group dominance at the expense of others. But it also should be noted that altruism can be a part of the model, as Dawkins has convincingly shown.[4] This approach is even consistent with ways by which reputation, trust, and other aspects of human behavior that on the surface appear to be altruistic and not consistent with individual wealth-maximization turn out to be superior survival traits under certain circumstances.[5]

Thus, we can build more elaborate models of complex human behavior within the individual expected-utility model, incorporating certain aspects of altruism. However an alternative approach, illustrated in Becker's study of the family (1981), explores altruism as still another facet of utility maximization, in which we get utility from the well-being of others. But this issue is deeper than family altruism. Both research in experimental economics and a number of studies by psychologists point out that issues of free-riding, fairness, and justice enter the utility function and do not necessarily fit neatly with the maximizing postulates in the narrow sense just described.[6] These issues appear to show in the voting behavior of legislators; it is widely observed that one cannot explain the voting behavior of legislators within the narrow confines of a principal/agent model, in which the agent (the legislator) is faithfully pursuing the interests of the principal (the constituents). The agent's own utility function – his or her own sense of the way the world ought to be – appears to play a role in the outcomes.

[4]See Dawkins, *The Selfish Gene* (1976).
[5]See, for example, R. Frank, "If Homo Economicus Could Choose His Own Utility Function Would He Want One with a Conscience?" (1987).
[6]See in particular the essay by Kahneman, Knetsch, and Thaler, "Fairness and the Assumptions of Economics" (1986); Richard Herrnstein, "A Behavioral Alternative to Utility Maximization" (1988), and Hoffman and Spitzer, "Entitlements, Rights and Fairness: Some Experimental Results" (1985).

The evidence we have with respect to ideologies, altruism, and self-imposed standards of conduct suggests that the trade-off between wealth and these other values is a negatively sloped function. That is, where the price to individuals of being able to express their own values and interests is low, they will loom large in the choices made; but where the price one pays for expressing one's own ideology, or norms, or preferences is extremely high, they will account much less for human behavior (Nelson and Silberberg, 1987). I shall come back to this point, because it helps us to understand a great deal, both about institutions and about the way in which they influence decision making. I intend to demonstrate that institutions basically alter the price individuals pay and hence lead to ideas, ideologies, and dogmas frequently playing a major role in the choices individuals make.

III

The second crucial element in our understanding human behavior is deciphering the environment. This issue plays little or no role in the standard economist's repertoire, although Lucas (1986) acknowledges that one does not get the consequences of rational expectation models without learning on the part of the players and indeed without the implication of stable equilibria and competition (the implication Winter derives), so that the choices and the alternatives become clearly known. On the face of it, the assumptions of stable equilibrium and knowledge about alternatives are quite attractive, because our lives are made up of routines in which the matter of choices appears to be regular, repetitive, and clearly evident, so that 90 percent of our actions in a day do not require much reflection. But in fact, it is the existence of an imbedded set of institutions that has made it possible for us not to have to think about problems or to make such choices. We take them for granted, because the structure of exchange has been institutionalized in such a way as to reduce uncertainty. As soon as we move away from choices involving personal and repetitive actions to making choices involving impersonal and non-repetitive exchanges the uncertainty about outcomes increases. The more complex and unique the issues we confront, the more uncertain the outcome. We simply do not possess theories to predict effectively the outcomes, and the information we receive in such circumstances frequently does not permit us to update our models to improve them. Herbert Simon has put the issues very well:

> If we accept values as given and consistent, if we postulate an objective description of the world as it really is, and if we assume that the decisionmaker's computational powers are unlimited, then two important consequences follow. First,

we do not need to distinguish between the real world and the decisionmaker's perception of it: He or she perceives the world as it really is. Second, we can predict the choices that will be made by a rational decisionmaker entirely from our knowledge of the real world and without a knowledge of the decisionmaker's perceptions or modes of calculation. (We do, of course, have to know his or her utility function.)

If, on the other hand, we accept the proposition that both the knowledge and the computational power of the decisionmaker are severely limited, then we must distinguish between the real world and the actor's perception of it and reasoning about it. That is to say, we must construct a theory (and test it empirically) of the processes of decision. Our theory must include not only the reasoning processes but also the processes that generate the actor's subjective representation of the decision problem, his or her frame.

The rational person in neo-classical economies always reaches the decision that is objectively, or substantively, best in terms of the given utility function. The rational person of cognitive psychology goes about making his or her decisions in a way that is procedurally reasonable in the light of the available knowledge and means of computation. (Simon, 1986, pp. S210–11)

Simon's statement captures the essence of why, in my view, the subjective and incomplete processing of information plays a critical role in decision making. It accounts for ideology, based upon subjective perceptions of reality, playing a major part in human beings' choices.[7] It brings into play the complexity and incompleteness of our information and the fumbling efforts we make to decipher it. It focuses on the need to develop regularized patterns of human interaction in the face of such complexities, and it suggests that these regularized interactions we call institutions may be very inadequate or very far from optimal in any sense of the term. In short, such a way of looking at how human beings proceed is consistent with the arguments about the formation of institutions, which I shall discuss later in this chapter.

In "The Origins of Predictable Behavior" (1983), Ronald Heiner makes many of the same points. He argues that the gap between the competence of the agent in deciphering problems and the difficulty in selecting the most preferred alternatives, what he calls the CD gap, is a major key to the way in which human beings behave. His essay is based upon the simple notion that the greater that gap, the more likely the agents will impose regularized and very limited patterns of response to be able to deal with the complexities and uncertainties associated with that gap. Heiner argues, indeed, that this uncertainty not only produces predictable behavior

[7]By ideology I mean the subjective perceptions (models, theories) all people possess to explain the world around them. Whether at the microlevel of individual relationships or at the macrolevel of organized ideologies providing integrated explanations of the past and present, such as communism or religions, the *theories* individuals construct are *colored* by normative views of how the world should be organized.

but is the underlying source of institutions. Heiner's essay is unique in its attempt to connect uncertainty and behavior with the creation of institutions. His framework is evolutionary, however, and leaves no room for subjective perceptions of fairness to enter into the behavioral decisions of individuals.

IV

We can summarize the issues discussed above by returning to the classic defense and reacting to the seven points Winter sets forth.

1. For some purposes the concept of equilibrium is a valuable tool of analysis, but for most of the issues that we are concerned with there is not one equilibrium, but multiple equilibria that arise because "there is a continuum of theories that agents can hold and act on without ever encountering events which lead them to change their theories" (Hahn, 1987, p. 324).

2. Although individual actors face many repetitious situations and, as noted above, can act rationally in such situations, they also are confronted with many unique and nonrepetitive choices where the information is incomplete and where outcomes are uncertain.

3. Although Becker and Stigler have made an impressive case (1977) for relative price changes accounting for many apparent changes in preferences, the stability issue is not so easily dismissed. Not only do anomalies show up at the disaggregated level at which psychological research has been conducted, but certainly historical evidence suggests that preferences over time change. I know of no way to explain the demise of slavery in the nineteenth century that does not take into account the changing perception of the legitimacy of one person owning another.

4. Actors would certainly like to improve outcomes, but the information feedback may be so poor that the actor cannot identify better alternatives.

5. Competition may be so muted and the signals so confused that adjustment may be slow or misguided and the classic evolutionary consequences may not obtain for very long periods of time.

6. The condition of the world throughout history provides overwhelming evidence of much more than simple rational noncooperative behavior.

7. The behavioral assumptions of economists are useful for solving certain problems. They are inadequate to deal with many issues confronting social scientists and are the fundamental stumbling block preventing an understanding of the existence, formation, and evolution of institutions.

V

It would be nice to conclude this chapter with a precise and tidy behavioral model that not only explained why institutions are a necessary extension of the way human beings process information, but also predicted the complex mix of motivations that shape choices. We have made progress toward doing so; indeed enough to explain the existence of institutions and (less precisely) the motivation of the actors that helps to shape institutions and provides the means by which altruism and other nonwealth-maximizing values enter the choice set.

Institutions exist to reduce the uncertainties involved in human interaction. These uncertainties arise as a consequence of both the complexity of the problems to be solved and the problem-solving software (to use a computer analogy) possessed by the individual. There is nothing in the above statement that implies that the institutions are efficient.

The complexity of the environment is the subject of the next chapter. It is sufficient to say here that the uncertainties arise from incomplete information with respect to the behavior of other individuals in the process of human interaction. The computational limitations of the individual are determined by the capacity of the mind to process, organize, and utilize information. From this capacity taken in conjunction with the uncertainties involved in deciphering the environment, rules and procedures evolve to simplify the process. The consequent institutional framework, by structuring human interaction, limits the choice set of the actors.

There can be no question that the mind's ability to process information is limited, but how does the motivation of the actor enter into the decision-making process? In a strict sociobiological model, maximizing survival potential motivates the actor. Such motivation sometimes, but not always, coincides with wealth-maximizing behavior. The complexity of the environment, given the limited processing ability of the actor, can explain the subjective perceptions of reality that characterize human understanding and even the sense of fairness or unfairness that the individual feels about the institutional environment. To take classic illustrations it is not hard to understand how an industrial proletarian could feel that he or she was being exploited by the bourgeoisie, or how the late-nineteenth-century U.S. farmer could feel the railroad was responsible for his plight. In both cases there were ready-made ideological constructs that explained and accounted for their plight. But the fact that individuals acted upon those perceptions to overcome the free-rider problem is more difficult to explain.

The broad range of human actions characterized by such activities as the anonymous free donation of blood, the dedication to ideological causes such as communism, the deep commitment to religious precepts, or even the sacrificing of one's life for abstract causes could all be dismissed (as many neoclassical economists dismiss them) if they were isolated events. But obviously they are not and they must be taken into account if we are to advance our understanding of human behavior. If our understanding of motivation is very incomplete, we can still take an important forward step by taking explicit account of the way institutions alter the price paid for one's convictions and hence play a critical role in the extent to which nonwealth-maximizing motivations influence choices. We will take such account in succeeding chapters. But first we must examine in detail what it is about the environment that is so complex.

4

A transaction cost theory of exchange

My theory of institutions is constructed from a theory of human behavior combined with a theory of the costs of transacting. When we combine them we can understand why institutions exist and what role they play in the functioning of societies. If we add a theory of production we can then analyze the role of institutions in the performance of economies.

The costliness of information is the key to the costs of transacting, which consist of the costs of measuring the valuable attributes of what is being exchanged and the costs of protecting rights and policing and enforcing agreements. These measurement and enforcement costs are the sources of social, political, and economic institutions. The rest of this chapter concentrates on economic exchange; in Chapter 6 I will build a model of political exchange from the same building blocks.

The costliness of economic exchange distinguishes the transaction costs approach from the traditional theory economists have inherited from Adam Smith. For 200 years the gains from trade made possible by increasing specialization and division of labor have been the cornerstone of economic theory. Specialization could be realized by increasing the size of markets, and as the world's economy grew and division of labor became ever more specific, the number of exchanges involved in the performance of economies expanded. But the long line of economists who built this approach into an elegant body of economic theory did so without regard to the costliness of this exchange process. An exchange process involving transaction costs suggests significant modifications in economic theory and very different implications for economic performance.[1]

---

[1] The transaction cost approach is consistent only in its agreement on the importance of transaction costs; it is far from unified in other respects. The approach developed here might most appropriately be characterized as the University of Washington approach, originated by Steven Cheung (1974, 1983) and elaborated, modified, and developed at the University of Washington, most notably by Yoram Barzel (1982, 1989) but also by Keith Leffler (with Klein, 1981), Masanori Hashimoto (1979), and

27

Wallis and North (1986), measuring the size of transaction costs that go through the market (such as costs associated with banking, insurance, finance, wholesale, and retail trade; or, in terms of occupations, with lawyers, accountants, etc.) in the U.S. economy found that more than 45 percent of national income was devoted to transacting and, moreover, that this percentage had increased from approximately 25 percent a century earlier. Thus the resources of the economy consumed in transacting are of considerable magnitude and growing. Because transaction costs are a part of the costs of production, we need to restate the traditional production relationship as follows. The total costs of production consist of the resource inputs of land, labor, and capital involved both in transforming the physical attributes of a good (size, weight, color, location, chemical composition, and so forth) and in transacting – defining, protecting, and enforcing the property rights to goods (the right to use, the right to derive income from the use of, the right to exclude, and the right to exchange).

Once we recognize that the costs of production are the sum of transformation and transaction costs, we require a new analytical framework of microeconomic theory.[2] However, our concern in this study is a theory of institutions, and although that focus inevitably overlaps with some fundamental issues in microeconomic theory, to explore systematically the implications for the latter theory would take us in another direction. Our initial question, however – why is it costly to transact? – is common both to the restructuring of microtheory and to a theory of institutions.

I

As we saw in Chapter 2, in "The Problem of Social Cost" (1960) Ronald Coase made clear that only in the absence of transaction costs did the neoclassical paradigm yield the implied allocative results; with positive transaction costs, resource allocations are altered by property rights structures. Neither Coase nor many of the subsequent studies of transaction costs have attempted to define precisely what it is about transacting that is so costly, but that issue is central to the issues of this study and I now turn to it. I begin by exploring the costliness of measurement (holding enforcement costs constant) and then in Section III examine the costs of enforcement.

We get utility from the diverse attributes of a good or service or, in the case of the performance of an agent, from the multitude of separate

Douglass North (1981, 1984). Other approaches, notably that of Oliver Williamson, will be contrasted with the approach developed here.

[2]For the beginning of such a theory, see Barzel (1989).

activities that constitute performance.[3] This means, in common sense terms, that when I consume orange juice, I get utility from the quantity of juice I drink, the amount of vitamin C it contains, and its flavor, even though the exchange itself consisted simply of paying $2.00 for fourteen oranges. Similarly, when I buy an automobile, I get a particular color, acceleration, style, interior design, leg room, gasoline mileage – all valued attributes, even though it is only an automobile I buy. When I buy the services of doctors, their skill and bedside manner and the time spent waiting in their offices are part of the purchase. When as chairman of an economies department I hire assistant professors, not only the quantity and quality (however measured) of their teaching and research output (again, however measured), but a multitude of other aspects of their performance are also hired: whether they prepare for and meet classes on time, provide external benefits to colleagues, cooperate in department affairs, do not abuse their positions vis-à-vis students, or call friends in Hong Kong at departmental expense. The value of an exchange to the parties, then, is the value of the different attributes lumped into the good or service. It takes resources to measure these attributes and additional resources to define and to measure rights that are transferred.

The transfers that occur with an exchange entail costs that result from both parties attempting to determine what the valued attributes of these assets are – attributes that, because of prohibitive measurement costs, have remained poorly delineated. Thus, as a buyer of oranges I attempt to purchase an amount of juice, an amount of vitamin C, and the flavor of oranges, even though what I purchased was simply fourteen oranges for $2.00. Similarly, when as a potential buyer I look at an automobile, I attempt to ascertain whether it has the attributes important to me in a car. The same holds for the purchase of a doctor's services, about which I try to ascertain information on skill, bedside manner, and office waiting time.

From the particulars in the foregoing illustrations we can generalize as follows: commodities, services, and the performance of agents have numerous attributes and their levels vary from one specimen or agent to another. The measurement of these levels is too costly to be comprehensive or fully accurate. The information costs in ascertaining the level of individual attributes of each unit exchanged underlie the costliness of this aspect of transacting. Even if all exchanging individuals had the same objective function (for example, jointly maximizing the wealth of a firm that employed them), there would still be the transaction costs involved in acquiring the necessary information about the levels of attributes of each exchange unit, the location of buyers (sellers), and so forth. But, in fact

---

[3]For this extension of consumer theory see Lancaster (1966), Becker (1965), Cheung (1974), and Barzel (1982), among others.

there are asymmetries of information among the players, and these and the underlying behavioral function of individuals in combination produce radical implications for economic theory and for the study of institutions.

I take up the issue of asymmetry first. In the foregoing illustrations, the seller of oranges knew much more about the valuable attributes of the oranges than the buyer, the used car dealer knew much more about the valued attributes of the car than the buyer (Akerlof, 1970), and the doctor knew much more about the quality of services and skill than the patient. Likewise, prospective assistant professors know much more about their work habits than does the department chairman or, to take another example, the purchaser of life insurance from an insurance company knows much more about his or her health than the insurer does.

Not only does one party know more about some valued attribute than the other party, he or she may stand to gain by concealing that information. According to a strictly wealth-maximizing behavioral assumption, a party to exchange will cheat, steal, or lie when the payoff to such activity exceeds the value of the alternative opportunities available to the party. Indeed, this assumption was the basis of Akerlof's famous article on lemons (1970), of the dilemmas posed by adverse selection in the purchase of life insurance, of problems of moral hazard (Holmstrom, 1979), and of a multitude of other issues that have emerged in the literature over the last dozen years in what is called the New Industrial Organization literature. Although it is sometimes in the interests of the exchanging parties to conceal certain kinds of information, at other times it is in their interests to reveal information. With this background we can develop some generalizations about the measurement aspects of a transaction cost model of exchange.

II

Consider first the standard neoclassical Walrasian model. In this general equilibrium model, commodities are identical, the market is concentrated at a single point in space, and the exchange is instantaneous. Moreover, individuals are fully informed about the exchange commodity and the terms of trade are known to both parties. As a result, no effort is required to effect exchange other than to dispense with the appropriate amount of cash. Prices, then, become a sufficient allocative device to achieve highest value uses.

To the Walrasian model, which includes the maximizing behavior of individuals, the gains that result from specialization, and the division of labor that produces exchange, I now add costs of information. As noted above, these include the costs of measuring the valued attributes of goods and services and the varying characteristics of the performance of agents. The net gains from exchange are the gross gains, which are the standard gains in neoclassical theory and in the international trade model, minus the costs of measuring and policing the agreement and minus the losses that result because monitoring is not perfect. On a common sense level, it is easy to see that we devote substantial resources and efforts to the measurement, enforcement, and the policing of agreements. Warranties, guarantees, trademarks, the resources devoted to sorting and grading, time and motion studies, the bonding of agents, arbitration, mediation, and of course the entire system of judicial process all reflect the ubiquity of measurement and enforcement.

Because it is costly to measure the valued attributes fully, the opportunity for wealth capture by devoting resources to acquiring more information is ever present. For example, the seller of a commodity such as fruits and vegetables may find it too costly to sort and grade them precisely. On the other hand, a buyer may find that it is worthwhile to devote time to picking and choosing among the fruit and vegetables available. In this case the seller has put into the public domain the variability of attributes that can in part be captured by the buyer devoting time and effort to sorting them out. The same can be said for the purchaser of a used automobile or the purchaser of medical services of doctors. Because of the enormous variety in the characteristics and the costliness of measuring attributes of goods and services and the performance of agents, the ideal ownership rights, with respect to these assets and resources, may take a variety of forms. In some cases, the ideal form is that the rights be divided among the parties. The buyer of a durable good, for example, may own some rights; others remain with the manufacturer in the form of guarantees of performance.

As a generalization, the more easily others can affect the income flow from someone's assets without bearing the full costs of their action, the lower is the value of that asset. As a result, the maximization of an asset's value involves the ownership structure in which those parties who can influence the variability of particular attributes become residual claimants over those attributes. In effect they are then responsible for their actions and have an incentive to maximize the potential gains from exchange. The rights to an asset generating a flow of services are usually easy to assure when the flow can be easily measured, because it is easy to impose a charge commensurate with a level of service. Therefore, when a flow is known and constant, it is easy to assure rights. If the flow varies but is predictable, rights are still easy to assure. When the flow of income from an asset can be affected by the exchange parties, assigning ownership becomes more problematic. When the income stream is variable and not fully predictable, it is costly to determine whether the flow is what it should be in that particular case. In such an instance, both parties will try to capture some part of the contestable income stream.

III

So far the emphasis of the analysis has been on measurement. It is, however, measurement plus the costliness of enforcement that together determine the costs of transacting. If we return to the Walrasian model described above, we assume that there are no costs associated with enforcement of agreements. Indeed, as long as we maintain the fiction of a unidimensional good transacted instantaneously, the problems of policing and enforcement are trivial. But when we add the costs of acquiring information and, specifically, of measuring, the problems become major ones. It is because we do not know the attributes of a good or service or all the characteristics of the performance of agents and because we have to devote costly resources to try to measure and monitor them that enforcement issues do arise.

One issue is that of policing agents. The most extreme example concerns the relationship between a master and slave. There is, in fact, an implicit contract between the two; to get maximum effort from the slave, the owner must devote resources to monitoring and metering a slave's output and critically applying rewards and punishments based on performance. Because there are increasing marginal costs to measuring and policing performance, the master will stop short of perfect policing and will engage instead in policing until the marginal costs equal the additional marginal benefits from such activity. The result is that slaves acquire certain property rights in their own labor. That is, owners are able to enhance the value of their property by granting slaves some rights in exchange for services the owners value more. Hence slaves became owners too. Indeed it is only this ownership that made it possible for slaves to purchase their own freedom, as was frequently done in classical times and even occasionally in the antebellum South.[4]

Although the slave example is an extreme form, the agency issue is ubiquitous in hierarchical organizations. The problems of monitoring and metering the various attributes that constitute performance of agents mean that, in contrast to the standard neoclassical frictionless model of workers being paid the value of their marginal product, they are paid this cost minus the resource costs of monitoring and policing.[5] In the above illustration I implicitly introduced property rights when I referred to the

---

[4]See Barzel (1977) for a detailed elaboration of this argument.
[5]Jensen and Meckling in a well-known essay (1976) have elaborated on the agency costs involved in monitoring, policing, and the shirking of agents.

concept of a master owning a slave; and in all discussions of principal/agents and the monitoring problem, we assume that the principal has the power of disciplining the agent and therefore of enforcing agreements. Likewise, the agent can monitor the principal and enforce his or her end of the agreement.

Enforcement can come from second-party retaliation. It also can result from internally enforced codes of conduct or by societal sanctions or a coercive third party (the state).

But one cannot take enforcement for granted. It is (and always has been) the critical obstacle to increasing specialization and division of labor. Enforcement poses no problem when it is in the interests of the other party to live up to agreements. But without institutional constraints, self-interested behavior will foreclose complex exchange, because of the uncertainty that the other party will find it in his or her interest to live up to the agreement. The transaction cost will reflect the uncertainty by including a risk premium, the magnitude of which will turn on the likelihood of defection by the other party and the consequent cost to the first party. Throughout history the size of this premium has largely foreclosed complex exchange and therefore limited the possibilities of economic growth.

IV

We are now ready to explore the relationship among the behavioral assumptions developed in Chapter 3, the characteristics of transacting as developed in the previous sections of this chapter, and the institutional structure of a society.

Property rights are the rights individuals appropriate over their own labor and the goods and services they possess. Appropriation is a function of legal rules, organizational forms, enforcement, and norms of behavior – that is, the institutional framework. Because with any property rights structure transaction costs are positive, rights are never perfectly specified and enforced; some valued attributes are in the public domain and it pays individuals to devote resources to their capture. Because the costs of transacting have changed radically throughout history and vary equally radically in different contemporary economies, the mix between the formal protection of rights and individual attempts to capture rights or devote resources to individual protection of their own rights varies enormously. We have only to compare property rights in Beirut in the 1980s with those of a modern small-town U.S. community to cover the spectrum. In the former, most valuable rights are in the public domain, to be seized by those with the violence potential to be successful; in the latter the legal structure defines and enforces a large share of rights and those valuable rights in the public domain tend to be allocated by traditional norms of behavior. The difference between these two is a function of the institutional structure in each.

Institutions provide the structure for exchange that (together with the technology employed) determines the cost of transacting and the cost of transformation. How well institutions solve the problems of coordination and production is determined by the motivation of the players (their utility function), the complexity of the environment, and the ability of the players to decipher and order the environment (measurement and enforcement).

The institutions necessary to accomplish economic exchange vary in their complexity, from those that solve simple exchange problems to ones that extend across space and time and numerous individuals. The degree of complexity in economic exchange is a function of the level of contracts necessary to undertake exchange in economies of various degrees of specialization. Nonspecialization is a form of insurance when the costs and uncertainties of transacting are high. The greater the specialization and the number and variability of valuable attributes, the more weight must be put on reliable institutions that allow individuals to engage in complex contracting with a minimum of uncertainty about whether the terms of the contract can be realized. Exchange in modern economies consisting of many variable attributes extending over long periods of time necessitates institutional reliability, which has only gradually emerged in Western economies. There is nothing automatic about the evolution of cooperation from simple forms of contracting and exchange to the complex forms that have characterized the successful economies of modern times.

Institutions structure economic exchange in an enormous variety of forms that do, however, fall into general types that are consistent with the transactions cost model of exchange. The kind of exchange that has characterized most of economic history has been personalized exchange involving small-scale production and local trade. Repeat dealing, cultural homogeneity (that is a common set of values), and a lack of third-party enforcement (and indeed little need for it) have been typical conditions. Under them transactions costs are low, but because specialization and division of labor is rudimentary, transformation costs are high. The economies or collections of trading partners in this kind of exchange tend to be small.

As the size and scope of exchange have increased, the parties have attempted to clientize or personalize exchange. But the greater the variety and numbers of exchange, the more complex the kinds of agreements that have to be made, and so the more difficult it is to do. Therefore a second general pattern of exchange has evolved, that is impersonal exchange, in which the parties are constrained by kinship ties, bonding, exchanging hostages, or merchant codes of conduct. Frequently the exchange is set within a context of elaborate rituals and religious precepts to constrain the participants. The early development of long-distance and cross-cultural trade and the fairs of medieval Europe were built on such institutional constructs. They permitted a widening of the market and the realization of the gains from more complex production and exchange, extending beyond the bounds of a small geographic entity. In early modern Europe, these institutions led to an increasing role of the state in protecting merchants and to the adoption of merchant codes as the revenue potential of such fiscal activities increased. However, in this environment the role of the state was at best ambiguous, because the state was as often an increasing source of insecurity and higher transaction costs as it was protector and enforcer of property rights.

The third form of exchange is impersonal exchange with third-party enforcement. It has been the critical underpinning of successful modern economies involved in the complex contracting necessary for modern economic growth. Third-party enforcement is never ideal, never perfect, and the parties to exchange still devote immense resources to attempting to clientize exchange relationships. But neither self-enforcement by parties nor trust can be completely successful. It is not that ideology or norms do not matter; they do and immense resources are devoted to attempting to promulgate codes of conduct. Equally, however, the returns on opportunism, cheating, and shirking rise in complex societies. A coercive third party is essential. One cannot have the productivity of a modern high income society with political anarchy. Indeed, effective third-party enforcement is best realized by creating a set of rules that then make a variety of informal constraints effective. Nevertheless, the problems of achieving third-party enforcement of agreements via an effective judicial system that applies, however imperfectly, the rules are only very imperfectly understood and are a major dilemma in the study of institutional evolution.

Thus, it should be readily apparent that to develop a model of institutions, we must explore in depth the structural characteristics of informal constraints, formal rules, and enforcement and the way in which they evolve. Then we shall be in a position to put them together to look at the overall institutional makeup of political/economic orders.

5

Informal constraints

In all societies from the most primitive to the most advanced, people impose constraints upon themselves to give a structure to their relations with others. Under conditions of limited information and limited computational ability, constraints reduce the costs of human interaction as compared to a world of no institutions. However, it is much easier to describe and be precise about the formal rules that societies devise than to describe and be precise about the informal ways by which human beings have structured human interaction. But although they defy, for the most part, neat specification and it is extremely difficult to develop unambiguous tests of their significance, they are important.

In the modern Western world, we think of life and the economy as being ordered by formal laws and property rights. Yet formal rules, in even the most developed economy, make up a small (although very important) part of the sum of constraints that shape choices; a moment's reflection should suggest to us the pervasiveness of informal constraints. In our daily interaction with others, whether within the family, in external social relations, or in business activities, the governing structure is overwhelmingly defined by codes of conduct, norms of behavior, and conventions. Underlying these informal constraints are formal rules, but these are seldom the obvious and immediate source of choice in daily interactions.

That the informal constraints are important in themselves (and not simply as appendages to formal rules) can be observed from the evidence that the same formal rules and/or constitutions imposed on different societies produce different outcomes. And discontinuous institutional change, such as revolution or military conquest and subjugation, certainly produces new outcomes. But what is most striking (although seldom observed, particularly by advocates of revolution) is the persistence of so many aspects of a society in spite of a total change in the rules. Japanese culture survived the U.S. occupation after World War II; the post-revolutionary U.S. society remained much as it had been in colonial times; Jews, Kurds, and endless other groups have persisted through centuries despite endless changes in their formal status. Even the Russian Revolution, perhaps the most complete formal transformation of a society we know, cannot be completely understood without exploring the survival and persistence of many informal constraints.

Where do informal constraints come from? They come from socially transmitted information and are a part of the heritage that we call culture. The way the mind processes information depends "upon the brain's ability to learn by being programmed with one or more elaborately structured natural languages that can code for perceptual, attitudinal and moral (behavioral) as well as factual information" (Johansson, 1988, p. 176). Culture can be defined as the "transmission from one generation to the next, via teaching and imitation, of knowledge, values, and other factors that influence behavior" (Boyd and Richerson, 1985, p. 2). Culture provides a language-based conceptual framework for encoding and interpreting the information that the senses are presenting to the brain.

Essentially the argument being made here is an extension of the argument of Chapter 3 that processing information is the key to understanding a more complex behavioral pattern than is derived from the expected utility model. But the emphasis in that chapter was on the incompleteness of the information and the consequent need for institutions to structure human interrelations. In this chapter the emphasis is on the way that the cultural filter provides continuity so that the informal solution to exchange problems in the past carries over into the present and makes those informal constraints important sources of continuity in long-run societal change.

I

I begin by examining human interaction when there are no formal rules. How is order preserved in stateless societies? The anthropological literature is extensive, and although many of the findings are still controversial, it makes important reading not only for the study of historical work and for an analysis of order in primitive societies, but also for its implications for a modern understanding of informal constraints. Robert Bates (1987), building his analysis on Evans-Pritchard's classic study of the Nuer, states the issue of such constraints as follows:

The puzzle, from Evans-Pritchard's point of view, was that, despite the potential for theft and disorder, the Nuer in fact tended to live in relative harmony. Insofar as the Nuer raided cattle, they tended to raid the cattle of others; raids within the tribe were relatively rare. Somehow the Nuer appear to have avoided the potentially harmful effects arising from the pursuit of self-interest. And they appear to have done so even while lacking those formal institutions so common in Western societies which specialize in preserving the peace and forestalling violence: the courts, the police, and so on. (Bates, 1987, p. 8)

Bates then describes the deterring effects that both compensation among the tribe and the threat of feud posed for preserving order. He shows how this cooperative solution makes sense in game theoretic terms. A one-shot prisoner's dilemma problem, where it would appear that the players must arrive at a violent solution with the result that each family is worse off, is avoided. Instead an iterated game is played, and with the threat of feud it is in the interests of the parties to preserve order and hence not to pursue interfamily cattle raiding. The critical point here is that it is the members of the family themselves who prevent other family members from engaging in raiding, because a feud, once started, would be harmful to all members.

The extensive literature that anthropologists have produced on primitive societies makes clear that exchange in tribal societies is not simple. In the absence of the state and formal rules, a dense social network leads to the development of informal structures with substantial stability. No one has described this situation better than Elizabeth Colson (1974).

Whether we call them customs, laws, usages, or normative rules seems of little importance. What is important is that communities such as the Tonga do not leave their members free to go their own way and explore every possible avenue of behavior. They operate with a set of rules or standards which define appropriate action under a variety of circumstances. The rules, by and large, operate to eliminate conflict of interests by defining what it is people can expect from certain of their fellows. This has the healthy effect of limiting demands and allowing the public to judge performance. . . .

At another level, however, they would see conflict as endemic to social life because people who live in close juxtaposition use the same space and want support and attention from the same individuals. Rules, even though they may at times produce conflict, reduce the chances for conflict because they reduce the total amount of ambiguity for those concerned by defining specific rather than universalistic claims and obligations. It becomes possible to order one's life with a set of priorities regarded as legitimate. . . . Among the Tonga I have had to learn that I should not give just because I feel like giving as this is an insult to all who do not receive. Rules do not solve all problems; they only simplify life.

They also give a framework for organizing activities. Standards and some means of applying sanctions are necessary complements to the rules if a system of social control is to operate within a community. Among people such as the Tonga, onlookers apply the standards of performance in particular roles in making an overall judgement [sic] about the total person; this in turn allows them to predict future behavior. Judgment is an ongoing process through which consensus is finally reached. (Colson, 1974, pp. 51–3)

Informal constraints

Several implications are clear from this review of work by Colson and other anthropologists. Order in the societies they describe is the result of a dense social network where people have an intimate understanding of each other and the threat of violence is a continuous force for preserving order because of its implications for other members of society. Deviant behavior cannot be tolerated in such a situation, because it is a fundamental threat to the stability and insurance features of the tribal group.

Richard Posner's model of primitive society (1980), which generates an explanation of many institutional features of such societies, is similar to the one I develop here (although mine has none of the maximizing social wealth or efficiency implications that are explicit in Posner's work). In Posner's model, high information costs, the absence of effective government, limited numbers of goods and limited trade, limited food preservation, and negligible gains from innovation produce a set of common characteristics:

Weak government, ascription of rights and duties on the basis of family membership, gift-giving as a fundamental mode of exchange, strict liability for injuries, emphasis on generosity and honor as high ethical norms, collective guilt – these and other features of social organization recur with such frequency in accounts of primitive and archaic societies as to suggest that a simple model of primitive society, which abstracts from many of the particular features of specific societies, may nonetheless explain much of the structure of primitive social institutions. (Posner, 1980, p. 8)

Posner's essay emphasizes the importance of kinship ties as the central insurance, protection, and law enforcement mechanisms of primitive societies. Bates' study of Kenya (1989) equally focuses on the changing pattern of kinship ties in the context of political/economic conditions as the key to understanding the evolving institutional constraints of a society in rapid transition from a tribal society to a market economy.

II

Informal constraints are pervasive features of modern economies as well. In order to dispel the assertion by law and economics scholars of the centrality of legal doctrine, Robert Ellickson did a field study of the way in which rural residents of Shasta County, California, resolved disputes arising over trespass damage done by stray livestock.[1] He found that the residents almost never resorted to legal redress, but instead relied on an elaborate structure of informal constraints to resolve disputes. In a subsequent article (1987) and forthcoming book, Ellickson provides a great

[1]Appropriately titled "Of Coase and Cattle: Dispute Resolution Among Neighbors in Shasta County" (1986).

deal of additional empirical evidence of the pervasiveness of informal constraints.

Even the most casual introspection suggests the pervasiveness of informal constraints. Arising to coordinate repeated human interaction, they are (1) extensions, elaborations, and modifications of formal rules, (2) socially sanctioned norms of behavior, and (3) internally enforced standards of conduct. I elaborate on each of these aspects of informal constraints.

1. In a study of the institutional foundations of committee power Shepsle and Weingast (1987) demonstrate that the power of congressional committees that is not explained by the formal rules is a result of a set of informal unwritten constraints that have evolved in the context of repeated interaction (exchange) among the players. These constraints evolved from the formal rules to deal with specific problems of exchange and became established as recognized institutional constraints even though they were never made a part of the formal rules. Committee chairs and committees consequently have an influence over legislative choices that could not be derived from the formal structure.

2. Robert Axelrod (1986) provides a vivid illustration of a socially sanctioned norm of behavior. The night before he was to engage in a duel with Aaron Burr, Alexander Hamilton sat down and wrote out all the reasons why he should not accept this challenge; a crucial one, of course, was that he was likely to get killed. Yet, in spite of the overwhelming rational bases for not dueling, he felt that his effectiveness in the public arena would be significantly diminished by such a decision because dueling was the accepted way to settle disputes among gentlemen. Social norms dictated the choice, not formal rules.

3. Both of the first two types of informal constraints can be modeled in the context of wealth-maximizing models and therefore lend themselves to treatment in neoclassical (and game theory) frameworks. But internally enforced codes of conduct only have meaning in terms of informal constraints, altering choices when the individual gives up wealth or income for some other value in his or her utility function. Numerous essays explore voting behavior by legislators and conclude that one cannot explain legislative voting behavior by an interest group model (in which the legislator faithfully mirrors the interests of his or her constituents), but must take into account the subjective, personal preferences of the legislator (Kalt and Zupan, 1984). This literature is controversial because of the statistical problems in getting unambiguous answers, but there is abundant qualitative and quantitative evidence that the lower the price of ideas, ideologies, and convictions, the more they matter and affect choices (for empirical support see Nelson and Silberberg, 1987).

III

How do we explain the emergence and persistence of informal constraints? A pervasive but relatively simple to explain form of such constraints is conventions that solve coordination problems: "These are rules that have never been consciously designed and that it is in everyone's interest to keep" (Sugden, 1986, p. 54). The usual illustration of such a convention is *rules* of the road. The important characteristic of conventions is that, given the costs of exchange (Chapter 4), both parties have a stake in minimizing the costliness of measurement and the exchanges are self-enforcing. In terms of the total resources that go into transacting in an economy, conventions that solve coordination probably account for a larger proportion of the costs of transacting than the other informal constraints described later in this chapter (although in many instances the transaction costs in fact reflect a combination of sources of informal constraints).

Informal constraints that arise in the context of exchange but are not self-enforcing are more complex because they necessarily entail features that make the exchange viable by reducing measurement and enforcement costs. In the absence of constraints, asymmetric information and the consequent distribution of the gains will lead to devoting excessive resources to measurement or indeed can lead to exchange not taking place at all because the exchange is unenforceable. Informal constraints can take the form of agreed upon lower cost forms of measurement (standardized weights and measures, for example) and make second- and third-party enforcement effective by specific sanctioning devices or information networks that acquaint third parties with exchange performance (credit ratings, better business bureaus, etc.). Such organizations and instruments that make norms of cooperative behavior (informal constraints) effective are not only a major part of the story of more complex exchange through history, but are strikingly paralleled by the game theoretic models that produce cooperative outcomes through features that alter discount rates and increase information. The growth of more complex forms of exchange in later medieval and early modern Europe was made possible by a variety of informal institutions such as the early law merchant's publicized codes of merchant conduct. Prices current and the development of auditing and accounting techniques lowered critical (i.e., measurable) information and enforcement costs. These can be modeled in a game theoretic framework by raising the gains from cooperative action or raising the costs of defecting (see Milgrom, North, and Weingast, 1990).

Much more difficult to deal with in theoretical terms than wealth maximizing informal constraints are internally enforced codes of conduct that modify behavior. It is difficult because one must devise a model that predicts choices in the context of the trade-off between wealth and other values. But strong religious beliefs or commitment to communism, for example, provide us with historical accounts of the sacrifices individuals have made for beliefs. As noted earlier, experimental economics provides evidence that individuals do not always free-ride and a study by Frank (1988) provides both a large body of evidence and a model of such behavior.

The literature cited above and the earlier chapter of this book dealing with human behavior make clear that motivation is more complicated than the simple expected utility model. Chapter 3 also emphasized that under certain conditions traits like honesty, integrity, and living up to a reputation pay off in strictly wealth-maximizing terms. Still unexplained is a very large residual. We simply do not have any convincing theory of the sociology of knowledge that accounts for the effectiveness (or ineffectiveness) of organized ideologies or accounts for choices made when the payoffs to honesty, integrity, working hard, or voting are negative.

Two partial explanations are Howard Margolis's (1982) dual utility model (mentioned in Chapter 2) and Robert Sugden's argument about conventions acquiring moral force. Margolis's argument is that individuals possess not one but two utility functions: S preferences are governed by the usual self-interest preference function, whereas G preferences are purely social (group interested). Margolis attempts to give empirical content to the argument by developing a model with assigned weights given self-interest preferences versus weights given group-interest preferences and by exploring the conditions under which the weights change. Sugden (1986) maintains that a convention acquires moral force when almost everyone in the community follows it, and it is in the interests of each individual that people with whom he or she deals follow the rule providing that the individual does too. What evolves according to Sugden is a "morality of cooperation" (Sugden, 1986, p. 173).

IV

It is time to pull together and summarize the argument of this chapter. The way by which the mind processes information not only is the basis for the existence of institutions, but is a key to understanding the way informal constraints play an important role in the makeup of the choice set both in the short-run and in the long-run evolution of societies.

In the short run, culture defines the way individuals process and utilize information and hence may affect the way informal constraints get specified. Conventions are culture specific, as indeed are norms. However norms pose some still unexplained problems. What is it that makes norms evolve or disappear – for example, dueling as a solution to gentlemanly differences?

Even if we do not possess a good explanation for social norms, we can model wealth-maximizing norms in a game theoretic context. That is, we can explore and test, empirically, what sorts of informal constraints are most likely to produce cooperative behavior or how incremental changes in such informal constraints will alter the game to increase (or decrease) cooperative outcomes. This approach may increase our understanding of the development of more complex forms of exchange, such as the early evolution of financial markets.[2]

A transaction cost framework equally offers promise of exploring informal constraints. Although the informal institutional constraints are not directly observable, the contracts that are written, and sometimes the actual costs of transacting, provide us with indirect evidence of changes in informal constraints. The striking decline in interest rates in the Dutch capital market in the seventeenth century and in the English capital market in the early eighteenth century provides evidence of the increasing security of property rights as a consequence of the effective interaction of a variety of both formal and informal institutional constraints. For example, the enforcement of contracts that evolved from merchant codes of behavior included ostracism of those who violated agreements and the eventual encoding of customary practices into the formal law.[3]

The importance of self-imposed codes of behavior in constraining maximizing behavior in many contexts also is evident. Our understanding of the source of such behavior is deficient, but we can frequently measure its significance in choices by empirically examining marginal changes in the cost of expressing convictions. Such analysis opens the door to explaining the power of subjective perceptions in affecting choices. If the demand function is negatively sloped (i.e., the lower the cost of expressing one's convictions the more important will the convictions be as a determinant of choice) and formal institutions make it possible for individuals to express preferences at little cost to themselves, then indeed the subjective preferences that individuals hold play a big part in determining choices. Voting, hierarchies that produce slack in the principal/agent relationship in legislatures, and lifetime tenure for judges are formal institutional constraints that lower the cost of acting on one's convictions.

It is simply impossible to make sense out of history (or contemporary

[2]For an interesting game theoretic application, see John Veitch, "Repudiations and Confiscations by the Medieval State" (1986).

[3]See Douglass C. North, "Institutions, Transaction Costs, and the Rise of Merchant Empires," in J. Tracy, editor, *The Political Economy of Merchant Empires,* Cambridge University Press (forthcoming).

economies) without recognizing the central role that subjective preferences play in the context of formal institutional constraints that enable us to express our convictions at zero or very little cost. Ideas, organized ideologies, and even religious zealotry play major roles in shaping societies and economies.

Nineteenth-century U.S. economic history, briefly described in Chapter 1, is full of illustrations. Whether we trace the history and consequences of the abolitionist movement, or examine the reasoning of Supreme Court justices that explicitly undergirded the decisions they handed down, or explore the organization, policies, and legislative enactments of the Greenback, Granger, and Populist movements of the U.S. farmer, they all only make sense in the context of subjective perceptions of the actors in the context of formal institutional structures that altered the price individuals paid for their convictions and hence enabled their choices to become effective.

In the first case the religious zealotry of the abolitionist groups that activated them to organize politically, together with the Northern electorate's growing conviction of the immorality of slavery and the 1860 election, led to the Civil War and the elimination of slavery (Fogel, 1989). In the second case the lifetime tenure specified for justices shielded them from interest group pressures and permitted – encouraged – them to vote their convictions. Their convictions were derived from their subjective construction of the issues. From the Marshall Court (1801 to 1835) to the Rehnquist Court, the justices have interpreted and reinterpreted essentially the same set of rules. The Court reverses itself 180 degrees over time because the judges' subjective modeling of the issues changes. The third case reflects farmers' persistent beliefs that they were being wronged by monetary policies, railroads, grain elevators, bankers, and others. They acted on these convictions by forming organizations with the objective of enacting *corrective* legislation first in state legislatures, then through the Populist party and the Democratic party in the U.S. Congress.

What determines how much people will pay to express and act on their convictions? We seldom know much about the elasticity of the function or shifts in the function, but we do have abundant evidence that the function is negatively sloped and that the price incurred for acting on one's convictions is frequently very low (and hence convictions are significant) in many institutional settings.

The long-run implication of the cultural processing of information that underlies informal constraints is that it plays an important role in the incremental way by which institutions evolve and hence is a source of path dependence. We still are a long way from having any neat models of cultural evolution (although see Cavalli-Sforza and Feldman, 1981, and Boyd and Richerson, 1985, for some interesting attempts), but we do know that cultural traits have tenacious survival ability and that most cultural changes are incremental.

Equally important is the fact that the informal constraints that are culturally derived will not change immediately in reaction to changes in the formal rules. As a result the tension between altered formal rules and the persisting informal constraints produces outcomes that have important implications for the way economies change, which is the subject of Part II.

6

Formal constraints

The difference between informal and formal constraints is one of degree. Envision a continuum from taboos, customs, and traditions at one end to written constitutions at the other. The move, lengthy and uneven, from unwritten traditions and customs to written laws has been unidirectional as we have moved from less to more complex societies and is clearly related to the increasing specialization and division of labor associated with more complex societies.[1]

The increasing complexity of societies would naturally raise the rate of return to the formalization of constraints (which became possible with the development of writing), and technological change tended to lower measurement costs and encourage precise, standardized weights and measures. The creation of formal legal systems to handle more complex disputes entails formal rules; hierarchies that evolve with more complex organization entail formal structures to specify principal/agent relationships. The general characteristics of the shift from status to contract have been amply discussed, but it is worth emphasizing the following.

Formal rules can complement and increase the effectiveness of informal constraints. They may lower information, monitoring, and enforcement costs and hence make informal constraints possible solutions to more

---

[1] For a lengthy and thoughtful discussion of what we mean by formal rules, see Elinor Ostrom (1986). Ostrom breaks down the rule structure into the following specifics: position rules that specify a set of positions and how many participants hold each position, boundary rules that specify how participants are chosen to hold these positions and how participants leave these positions, scope rules that specify the set of outcomes that may be affected and the external inducements and/or costs assigned to each of these outcomes, authority rules that specify the set of actions assigned to a position at a particular node, aggregation rules that specify the decision functions to be used at a particular node to map action into intermediate or final outcomes, and information rules that authorize channels of communication among participants in positions and specify the language and form in which the communication will take place.

how does this
fit w/ budget rules?

46

typology of rules

complex exchange (see Milgrom, North, and Weingast, 1990, and Chapter 7 for elaboration). Formal rules also may be enacted to modify, revise, or replace informal constraints. A change in the bargaining strength of parties may lead to an effective demand for a different institutional framework for exchange, but the informal constraints stand in the way of accomplishing it. Sometimes (but not always) it is possible to supersede the existing informal constraints with new formal rules (this point will be elaborated and qualified in Chapter 10).

I

Formal rules include political (and judicial) rules, economic rules, and contracts. The hierarchy of such rules, from constitutions, to statute and common laws, to specific bylaws, and finally to individual contracts defines constraints, from general rules to particular specifications. And typically constitutions are designed to be more costly to alter than statute laws, just as a statute law is more costly to alter than individual contracts. Political rules broadly define the hierarchical structure of the polity, its basic decision structure, and the explicit characteristics of agenda control. Economic rules define property rights, that is the bundle of rights over the use and the income to be derived from property and the ability to alienate an asset or a resource. Contracts contain the provisions specific to a particular agreement in exchange.

Given the initial bargaining strength of the decision-making parties, the function of rules is to facilitate exchange, political or economic. The existing structure of rights (and the character of their enforcement) defines the existing wealth-maximizing opportunities of the players, which can be realized by forming either economic or political exchanges. Exchange involves bargains made within the existing set of institutions, but equally the players at times find it worthwhile to devote resources to altering the more basic structure of the polity to reassign rights.

The extent of economic and political diversity of interests will, given relative bargaining strength, influence the rules' structure. The immediate reason is that the more numerous the interests, the less likely the simple majority (in the polity) will obtain and the more likely exchange will be structured to facilitate complex forms of exchange (partly formal but also partly informal) and other ways of solving problems by coalition formation. It is important to note, however, that the function of formal rules is to promote certain kinds of exchange but not all exchange. Thus Madison, in *Federalist Paper Number 10*, maintained that the constitutional structure was devised in 1787 not only to facilitate certain kinds of exchange, but also to raise the costs of those kinds of exchange that promote the interests of factions. Similarly, in economic exchange patent laws and

47

trade secret laws are designed to raise the costs of those kinds of exchange deemed to inhibit innovation.

Before going further, it is important to stress that there is nothing in my argument so far about rules that implies efficiency. As stressed above, rules are, at least in good part, devised in the interests of private well-being rather than social well-being. Hence, rules that deny franchise, restrict entry, or prevent factor mobility are everywhere evident. This is not to deny that ideas and norms matter, but to establish that as a first approximation, rules are derived from self-interest.

Rules are generally devised with compliance costs in mind, which means that methods must be devised to ascertain that a rule has been violated, to measure the extent of the violation (and consequent damages to the party to exchange), and to apprehend the violator. The costs of compliance include measuring the multiple attributes of the goods or services being exchanged and measuring the performance of agents. In many cases, the costs of measurement, given the technology of the time, exceed the gains, and rules are not worth devising and ownership rights are not delineated. Changes in technology or relative prices will alter the relative gains from devising rules.

With these generalizations as background, we can now use the framework derived from Chapters 3 and 4 to describe more closely political rules, property rights (economic rules), and contracts.

II

Broadly speaking, political rules in place lead to economic rules, though the causality runs both ways. That is, property rights and hence individual contracts are specified and enforced by political decision-making, but the structure of economic interests will also influence the political structure. In equilibrium, a given structure of property rights (and their enforcement) will be consistent with a particular set of political rules (and their enforcement). Changes in one will induce changes in the other. But because of the priority of political rules, we will analyze the structure of the political system first.

We start with a simplified model of a polity made up of a ruler and constituents.[2] In such a simple setting, the ruler acts like a discriminating monopolist, offering to different groups of constituents protection and justice or at least the reduction of internal disorder and the protection of property rights in return for tax revenue. Because different constituent groups have different opportunity costs and bargaining power with the

---

[2]This simple model is developed in much more detail in Chapter 3, "A Neo-classical Theory of the State" in North (1981).

ruler, different bargains result. But there are also economies of scale in the provision of these (semipublic) goods of law and enforcement. Hence, total revenue is increased, but the division of incremental gains between ruler and constituents depends on their relative bargaining power; changes at the margin, either the violence potential of the ruler or the opportunity costs of the constituent, will result in redivisions of the incremental revenue. Moreover, the ruler's gross and net revenue differ significantly as a result of the necessity of developing agents (a bureaucracy) to monitor, meter, and collect the revenue. All the consequences inherent to agency theory obtain here.

This model of the polity becomes one step more complicated when we introduce the concept of a representative body reflecting the interests of constituent groups and their role in bargaining with the ruler. This concept, consistent with the origin of parliaments, estates general, and cortes in early modern Europe, reflects the needs of the ruler to get more revenue in exchange for which he or she agrees to provide certain services to constituent groups. The representative body facilitates exchange between the parties. On the ruler's side, this leads to the development of a hierarchical structure of agents, which is a major transformation from the simple (if extensive) management of the king's household and estates to a bureaucracy monitoring the wealth and/or income of the king's constituents.

When we move from the historical character of representation in early modern Europe to modern representative democracy, our story is complicated by the development of multiple interest groups and by a much more complicated institutional structure devised to facilitate (again given relative bargaining strength) the exchange between interest groups.[3] This political transaction cost analysis is built on the recognition of the multiplicity of interest groups reflecting concentrations of voters in particular locations. Thus in the United States polity, there are elderly in Florida and Arizona, miners in Pennsylvania and West Virginia, artichoke growers in California, automobile manufacturers in Michigan, and so forth. Because

[3]The development of political theory in the last twenty-five years has paralleled developments in economic theory. The developments began in an a-institutional setting, in which the model paralleled the a-institutional model of economics. But the result, in terms of the formal theory, was that no stable equilibrium would evolve and that *cycling* would be a continuous pattern of political systems (at least in two-party, nonideological models). However, this formal finding was at odds with empirical and descriptive studies that provided no evidence of such disequilibrating characteristics, and it remained to take a further step in political theory to explore the nature of the institutional structure that provided for the evolution of equilibrium states in the political system. For a description of this evolution and a model of structure-induced equilibrium, see Kenneth Shepsle, "Institutional Equilibrium and Equilibrium Institutions" (1986).

there are multiple interest groups, no particular interest group that a legislator may represent can form a majority. Therefore, legislators cannot succeed acting alone, but must make agreements with other legislators, with different interests.

What kinds of institutions will evolve from exchange relationships between legislators reflecting multiple interest groups? Previous work, beginning with Buchanan and Tullock (1962), focused on vote-trading or logrolling. This approach was a step forward in recognizing the way by which legislators can strike bargains that facilitate exchange; however, it is too simple to solve fundamental problems involved in legislative exchange. It assumes that all bills and payoffs were known in advance, and it has a timeless dimension to it. In fact, a variety of exchanges arise in which today's legislation can only be enacted by commitments made for a future date. To lower the costs of exchange, it was necessary to devise a set of institutional arrangements that would allow for exchange over space and time. As with the economic exchange described in Chapter 4, the problem is to measure and enforce the exchange of rights.

How does credible commitment evolve to enable agreements to be reached when the payoffs are in the future and on completely different issues? Self-enforcement is important in such exchange, and in repeat dealings a reputation is a valuable asset. But as in economic exchange, the costs of measurement and enforcement, discovering who is cheating whom, when free-riding will occur, and who should bear the cost of punishing defectors make self-enforcement ineffective in many situations. Hence political institutions constitute ex ante agreements about cooperation among politicians. They reduce uncertainty by creating a stable structure of exchange. The result is a complicated system of committee structure, consisting of both formal rules and informal methods of organization. The evolution of this structure in the U.S. Congress is described in a recent study of the structure by Barry Weingast and William Marshall entitled "The Industrial Organization of Congress" (1988). In their conclusion, Weingast and Marshall specify the kind of structure that evolved:

Instead of trading votes, legislators exchanged special rights affording the holder of these rights additional influence over well-defined policy jurisdictions. This influence stems from the property rights established over the agenda mechanisms, that is, the means by which alternatives arise for votes. The extra influence over particular policies institutionalizes a specific pattern of trades. When the holders of seats on committees are precisely those individuals who would bid for votes on these issues in a market for votes, policy choice under the committee system parallels that under a more explicit exchange system. Because the exchange is institutionalized, it need not be renegotiated each new legislative session, and it is subject to fewer enforcement problems. (Weingast and Marshall, 1988, p. 157)

Formal constraints

The evolution of polities from single absolute rulers to democratic governments is typically conceived as a move toward greater political efficiency. In the sense that democratic government gives a greater and greater percentage of the populace access to the political decision-making process, eliminates the capricious capacity of a ruler to confiscate wealth, and develops third-party enforcement of contracts with an independent judiciary, the result is indeed a move toward greater political efficiency. But it would be wrong to assert that the result is efficient political markets in the same sense as we mean efficient economic markets. The existence of efficient economic markets entails competition so strong that, via arbitrage and information feedback, one approximates the Coase zero transaction cost conditions. Such markets are scarce enough in the economic world and even scarcer in the political world. It is true that the move toward a democratic polity will reduce legislative transaction costs per exchange (as elaborated by Weingast and Marshall, 1988), but not only will the number of exchanges increase so that the size of the total political transaction sector will grow, the agency costs between constituent and legislator and legislator and bureaucrat will be substantial. Moreover, *rational ignorance* on the part of constituents is going to increase the role, in many situations, of incomplete subjective perceptions playing an important part in choices. The atypical informed constituent may indeed know his or her own interest in making choices about familiar *local* repeated problems, but even the informed constituent is going to be at sea in making choices about the complex nonrepetitive problems of an interdependent political and economic world. The point is that formal political rules, like formal economic rules, are designed to facilitate exchange but democracy in the polity is not to be equated with competitive markets in the economy. The distinction is important with respect to the efficiency of property rights.

III

As a first approximation we can say that property rights will be developed over resources and assets as a simple cost-benefit calculus of the costs of devising and enforcing such rights, as compared to the alternatives under the status quo. Changes in relative prices or relative scarcities of any kind lead to the creation of property rights when it becomes worthwhile to incur the costs of devising such rights. This simple model has been the basis not only for my own early work (North and Thomas, 1973) but also for a substantial amount of the property rights literature, which looks on the development of property rights as a simple function of changes in economic costs and benefits. The simple model of the evolution of property rights would be consistent with Axelrod's *The Evolution of Coopera-*

tion (1984), but such an argument leaves out the role of the polity and the consequent kinds of property rights that will be specified and enforced.

In North (1981), I revised the 1973 argument to account for the obvious persistence of inefficient property rights. These inefficiencies existed because rulers would not antagonize powerful constituents by enacting efficient rules that were opposed to their interests or because the costs of monitoring, metering, and collecting taxes might very well lead to a situation in which less efficient property rights yielded more tax revenue than efficient property rights. This argument is an improvement over the efficiency argument but needs amplification.

The efficiency of the political market is the key to this issue. If political transaction costs are low and the political actors have accurate models to guide them, then efficient property rights will result. But the high transaction costs of political markets and subjective perceptions of the actors more often have resulted in property rights that do not induce economic growth, and the consequent organizations may have no incentive to create more productive economic rules. At issue is not only the incremental character of institutional change, but also the problem of devising institutions that can provide credible commitment so that more efficient bargains can be struck. In Chapter 11, I shall explore how such sufficient paths of development can persist through time.

IV

The rules descend from polities to property rights to individual contracts. Contracts will reflect the incentive-disincentive structure imbedded in the property rights structure (and the enforcement characteristics); thus the opportunity set of the players and the forms of organization they devise in specific contracts will be derived from the property rights structure.

The contract specified by economic theory is simple, complete, and straightforward. It involves an exchange of a unidimensional product at an instant of time. The contract in modern complex economies both is multidimensional and extends over time. Because there are multiple dimensions, with respect both to the physical characteristics and to the property rights characteristics of the exchange, of necessity the result is that one must spell out many of the provisions. Moreover, the contract will typically be incomplete, in the sense that there are so many unknowns over the life of contracts extending over time that the parties will (deliberately) leave to the courts or to some third party the settlement of disputes that arise over the life of the contract.[4]

---

[4] See Goldberg (1976) for discussion of relational exchange and the complicated contracts that in fact characterize modern exchange.

Formal constraints

Contracts provide not only an explicit framework within which to derive empirical evidence about the forms of organization (and hence are the basic empirical source for testing hypotheses about organization), but also clues with respect to the way by which the parties to an exchange will structure more complex forms of organization. That is, the contracts will reflect different ways to facilitate exchange, whether through firms, franchising, or other more complex forms of agreement that extend in a continuum from straightforward market exchange to vertically integrated exchange.[5] The complex interaction of institutional constraints and the development of organizations are the subject of Chapter 9.

I should close this chapter with a word of warning – although explicit rules provide us with a basic source of empirical materials by which to test the performance of economies under varying conditions, the degree to which these rules have unique relationships to performance is limited. That is, a mixture of informal norms, rules, and enforcement characteristics together defines the choice set and results in outcomes. Looking only at the formal rules themselves, therefore, gives us an inadequate and frequently misleading notion about the relationship between formal constraints and performance.

---

[5]The enormous literature that has evolved in the last fifteen or twenty years in the New Industrial Organization has provided us with an immense amount of valuable material on the kinds of organizations that will evolve and the forms of governance that will be reflected as ways to solve problems of complicated exchange. See in particular Oliver Williamson, *Markets and Hierarchies* (1975), and the subsequent literature that has developed from Williamson's pioneering work.

7

Enforcement

A good deal of literature on transaction costs takes enforcement as a given, assuming either that it is perfect or that it is *constantly* imperfect. In fact, enforcement is seldom either, and the structure of enforcement mechanisms and the frequency and severity of imperfection play a major role in the costs of transacting and in the forms that contracts take. There are two reasons why enforcement is typically imperfect. The first takes us back to the preceding chapters that explore the costs of measuring the multiple margins that constitute contract performance. The second rests in the fact that enforcement is undertaken by agents whose own utility functions influence outcomes.

In Chapter 4, asymmetries of information held by principals and agents about the valuable attributes of what was being exchanged were examined in the context of the wealth-maximizing behavior of the parties to exchange. In this chapter I wish to extend that analysis to explore the problems that arise in the transfer of rights. Parties to an exchange must be able to enforce compliance at a (transaction) cost such that the exchange is worthwhile to them. On the face of it, the problem sounds simple. Surely the gains from trade, which economists take to be the bedrock of economic performance, should make it worthwhile to evolve cooperative solutions among parties to capture jointly those gains. Indeed under certain circumstances, as I have noted in earlier chapters, the issues are so resolved. Trade does exist, even in *stateless* societies. Yet, as emphasized earlier, the inability of societies to develop effective, low-cost enforcement of contracts is the most important source of both historical stagnation and contemporary underdevelopment in the Third World.[1]

---

[1]This emphasis upon enforcement is another major difference between Oliver Williamson's approach to transaction costs and the one taken in this study. Williamson assumes enforcement to be imperfect (otherwise opportunism would never pay), but does not make it an explicit variable in his analysis. Such an approach simply does not lead the scholar to be able to deal with the problems of historical evolution, where

Enforcement

I

Under what conditions will contracts tend to be self-enforcing? In a wealth-maximizing world, the answer can be stated very simply. Contracts will be self-enforcing when it pays the parties to live up to them – that is, in terms of the costliness of measuring and enforcing agreements, the benefits of living up to contracts will exceed the costs. The most likely and indeed empirically observable state in which contracts are self-enforcing is that in which the parties to exchange have a great deal of knowledge about each other and are involved in repeat dealings, as detailed in the earlier chapter dealing with tribal and primitive societies and with small communities. Under these conditions, it simply pays to live up to agreements. In such a world, the measured costs of transacting are very low because of a dense social network of interaction. Cheating, shirking, opportunism, all problems of modern industrial organization, are limited or indeed absent because they do not pay. Norms of behavior determine exchange and formal contracting does not exist.

At the other extreme, the world of impersonal exchange is characterized by specialized interdependence in which the well-being of individuals depends upon the complex structure characterized by individual specialization and hence exchange extends through both time and space. In a pure model of the world of impersonal exchange, goods and services or the performance of agents is characterized by many valued attributes, exchange takes place over time, and there are no repeat dealings. In the context of a wealth-maximizing world, where there are high costs of measurement and no form of enforcement is possible, the gains from cheating and reneging exceed the gains from cooperative behavior. I have stated, of course, an extreme form of impersonal exchange, because in the real world, whether present or past (where impersonal exchange did occur to a degree), we find all kinds of mitigating circumstances by which parties attempt to assure compliance. The exchange of hostages, ostracism of merchants who reneged on agreements, to name two examples, provide incentives to parties to live up to agreements. Reputations, depending on the costs of information, provided parties in long-distance trade and impersonal exchange a mechanism to enforce agreements. Kinship ties, various forms of loyalty, minority groups in societies bound together by common beliefs in a hostile world – all provided frameworks within which living up to agreements was worthwhile. In addition, it should be noted that at times and places ideological commitments to integrity and honesty also played a major role. Nevertheless, the dilemma

the key problems of institutional change, of contracting, and of performance turn on the degree to which contracts can be enforced between parties at low cost.

that is posed by impersonal exchange without effective third-party enforcement is central to the major issues of development.

II

Let me explain this dilemma more precisely by expanding on the game theory framework briefly outlined in Chapter 2.[2] There I started with a very simple prisoner's dilemma situation in which it simply did not pay parties in a single exchange or in a single agreement to live up to the terms of exchange. Under these conditions, rational self-interested individuals will arrive at a Pareto inferior solution, that is, one that leaves both parties worse off than they would have been had they cooperated, because it is determined by one of the parties that he or she will be much worse off if the other party chooses not to cooperate. Now, there are ways for the parties to get around such a dilemma. They might ex ante sign a contract agreeing to live up to some set of standards, and they might hire lawyers to see that the contract is enforced. Note that by so doing, however, they have introduced transaction costs to the argument. And the costs of transacting, that is of providing the mechanism for assuring that the parties live up to a cooperative solution, may exceed the gains that the parties can derive from it.

If we shift from a once and for all game to a repeated game or an iterated game, then the possibility of a cooperative solution becomes much more evident, as Axelrod has explored (1984). That is, if the game continues indefinitely, it usually pays the parties to live up to the terms of exchange, because the gains from successive iterations exceed the benefits that could be derived from a single defection, from "running off with the profits." Note, however, that a game so conceived must be played in perpetuity. If there is an end of the game or people believe that the game might end, then indeed the discount rate may enter in to determining whether it is worthwhile to continue to cooperate. The smaller the probability of continuing for another round, the greater must be the payoffs to sustain an equilibrium; also, the greater the possibility of short-run gains, the greater must be the payoffs. Note that if the game runs continuously, there are still transaction costs, because one must still acquire information about the other party. However, the assumptions that are involved in this cooperative solution are seldom realized in the real world. They entail the game lasting continuously, they entail that one repeats the game with the

[2]This section depends heavily upon a substantial literature in game theory of which the essay "Corporate Culture and Economic Theory" by David M. Kreps (forthcoming in Alt and Shepsle, editors, *Perspectives on Positive Political Economy*) was especially useful.

same players, and they entail that one can observe compliance on the part of the other party. Observing compliance in terms of the model suggests that one can measure unambiguously the outcomes of contracts, so that one can determine whether a party has in fact not lived up to the terms of the contract.

This evolving story of game theory tells us that under very simplified conditions, that is, when the parties acquire perfect information and the game both lasts indefinitely into the future and is played between the same parties, one can reach self-enforcing cooperative solutions. But needless to say, these assumptions not only are strong but are simply not observed in the real world. In a world of impersonal exchange, we are exchanging with multiple individuals and can acquire very little information about all of them. Our information not only is imperfect, but varies remarkably from one party to another. Many times the exchange is a once and for all exchange and not repeated at all. Under these conditions, it is easy to see why the problems that we have laid out here are simply unresolvable in terms of cooperative solutions that can exist in impersonal exchange. The inevitable conclusion that one arrives at in a wealth-maximizing world is that complex contracting that would allow one to capture the gains from trade in a world of impersonal exchange must be accompanied by some kind of third-party enforcement. Indeed, this conclusion clearly mirrors the quotation from Norman Schofield at the end of Chapter 2, describing the conditions necessary for equilibrium solutions to emerge in the context of complex, cooperative games.

This game theoretic story can be translated into the framework developed in the preceding chapters. In the straightforward neoclassical story, the gains from trade are realized with zero transaction costs. That is, the parties to exchange costlessly know everything about the other party and enforcement is perfect. No institutions are necessary in a world of complete information. With incomplete information, however, cooperative solutions will break down unless institutions are created that provide sufficient information for individuals to police deviations. There are two parts to an institution's assuring cooperation. First, it is necessary to form a communications mechanism that provides the information necessary to know when punishment is required. By making available the relevant information, institutions make possible the policing of defections. Typically they economize on information, so, for example, players need no longer know the entire past history of any partner. Second, because punishment is often a public good in which the community benefits but the costs are borne by a small set of individuals, institutions must also provide incentives for those individuals to carry out punishment when called on to do so (see Milgrom, North, and Weingast, 1990, for an elaboration of this argument). It should be stressed that creating an institutional environment that induces credible commitment entails the complex institutional framework of formal rules, informal constraints, and enforcement that together make possible low-cost transacting.

This argument states that the players may devise an institutional framework to improve measurement and enforcement and therefore make possible exchange, but the resultant transaction costs raise the costs of exchange above the neoclassical level. The more resources that must be devoted to transacting to assure cooperative outcomes, the more diluted are the gains from trade of the neoclassical model. The more complex the exchange in time and space, the more complex and costly are the institutions necessary to realize cooperative outcomes. Quite complex exchange can be realized by creating third-party enforcement via voluntary institutions that lower information costs about the other party; ultimately, however, viable impersonal exchange that would realize the gains from trade inherent in the technologies of modern interdependent economies requires institutions that can enforce agreements by the threat of coercion. The transaction costs of a purely voluntary system of third-party enforcement in such an environment would be prohibitive. In contrast there are immense scale economies in policing and enforcing agreements by a polity that acts as a third party and uses coercion to enforce agreements. But therein lies the fundamental dilemma of economic development. If we cannot do without the state, we cannot do with it either. How does one get the state to behave like an impartial third party?

III

If formal third-party enforcement is essential, it is important to define exactly what one means by it. In principle, third-party enforcement would involve a neutral party with the ability, costlessly, to be able to measure the attributes of a contract and, costlessly, to enforce agreements such that the offending party always had to compensate the injured party to a degree that made it costly to violate the contract. These are strong conditions that obviously are seldom, if ever, met in the real world. It is costly to measure the attributes. The enforcer is an agent and has his or her own utility function, which will dictate his or her perceptions about the issues and therefore will be affected by his or her own interests. Enforcement is costly. Indeed, it is frequently costly even to find out that a contract has been violated, more costly to be able to measure the violation, and still more costly to be able to apprehend and impose penalties on the violator.

But achieving third-party enforcement in contracting is a major dilemma for economies that would engage in impersonal exchange. The development of credible commitment on the part of political bodies, such that one has assurances that political bodies will not violate contracts of parties or engage in conditions that will alter radically the wealth and income of parties, is always relative; even in the most highly developed countries we observe political entities altering the wealth of parties by all manner of changes in the price level or in rules that affect the well-being of individuals. Nevertheless, there is an immense difference in the degree to which we can rely upon contract enforcement between developed countries and Third World countries.

In developed countries, effective judicial systems include well-specified bodies of law and agents such as lawyers, arbitrators, and mediators, and one has some confidence that the merits of a case rather than private payoffs will influence outcomes. In contrast, enforcement in Third World economies is uncertain not only because of ambiguity of legal doctrine (a measurement cost), but because of uncertainty with respect to behavior of the agent.

Even when enforcement is sufficient to enable elaborate contracts to be made because they are subject to a system of courts that act as a bulwark against the violation of contracts, contractors must take into account those margins at which it is hard to measure whether a contract has been fulfilled. Hence, under conditions of uncertainties with respect to the future or problems of agency for which enforcement is difficult, the contracting parties will attempt to structure contracts that will minimize the potential both for contract violation and for rent dissipation by the parties.[3]

I conclude this analysis of enforcement by pointing out where it is taking us. Third-party enforcement means the development of the state as a coercive force able to monitor property rights and enforce contracts effectively, but no one at this stage in our knowledge knows how to create such an entity. Indeed, with a strictly wealth-maximizing behavioral assumption it is hard even to create such a model abstractly. Put simply, if the state has coercive force, then those who run the state will use that force in their own interest at the expense of the rest of the society. Madison laid out a solution to this problem in *The Federalist Papers* and Vincent Ostrom has expanded on it in his theory of the compound republic (1971); the correct constitutional forms will restrain the tyrannical exercise of political power. William Riker's skepticism, however, still seems appropriate:

But another main theme is a celebration of the efficacy of constitutional forms in restraining the tyrannical exercise of political power. This is the theme I wish to

[3]See Barzel (1982) for an elaboration of these issues.

address. I guess I want to defend the view he attributes to Woodrow Wilson. My initial tendency, however, as a constitutional theorist raised in the same tradition as Professor Ostrom has always been to agree with his proposition. But everytime I convince myself that I have found an instance in which constitutional forms do make a difference for liberty, my discovery comes apart in my hand. It is, of course, all a matter of the direction of causality. Professor Ostrom believes that at least part of the reason we are a free people is that we have certain constitutional forms; but it may just as easily be the case that the reason we have these constitutional forms is that we are a free people. The question is: Does constitutional structure cause a political condition and a state of public opinion or does the political condition and a state of public opinion cause the constitutional structure? This sounds at first like the chicken and egg problem in which there is no causal direction; but I think that usually there is a cause and that constitutional forms are typically derivative. It seems probable to me that public opinion usually causes constitutional structure, and seldom, if ever, the other way around. As Rousseau contended, it is in the end the law that is written in the hearts of the people that counts. (Riker, 1976, p. 13)

In a subsequent historical chapter, I briefly describe the way in which such constitutional forms evolved in England in the seventeenth century. But although that story describes a successful outcome, it does not give a definitive answer to the question of how it was achieved. It was surely a mixture of formal and informal constraints. Both respect for the law and the honesty and integrity of judges are an important part of this success story. They are self-enforcing standards of conduct, and I believe that they are important. How does one create such self-enforcing constraints? Part of the answer is that creating a system of effective enforcement and of moral constraints on behavior is a long, slow process that requires time to develop if it is to evolve – a condition markedly absent in the rapid transformation of Africa from tribal societies to market economies. The quote from William Riker goes to the heart of the issue of creating effective institutional constraints.

8

Institutions and transaction and transformation costs

It takes resources to define and protect property rights and to enforce agreements. Institutions together with the technology employed determine those transaction costs. It takes resources to transform inputs of land, labor, and capital into the output of goods and services and that transformation is a function not only of the technology employed, but of institutions as well. Therefore, institutions play a key role in the costs of production.

In previous chapters I specified why it is costly to transact and examined the variety of forms that institutional constraints take in constraining human interaction. Still ahead (in Chapter 9), I shall explore the way by which learning and organizations can modify and alter the relationship between institutions and transaction costs (and transformation costs as well). But first, I simply wish to pull together the threads of the argument so far.

A hierarchy of rules – constitutional, statute law, common law (and even bylaws) – together will define the formal structure of rights in a specific exchange. Moreover, a contract will be written with enforcement characteristics of exchange in mind. Because of the costliness of measurement, most contracts will be incomplete; hence informal constraints will play a major roles in the actual agreement. These will include reputation, broadly accepted standards of conduct (effective to the extent that the conduct of the other parties is readily observable), and conventions that emerge from repetitive interactions. The relationship between rights and constraints in an exchange can be illustrated at three levels: first at the level of a single straightforward exchange, second in the more complex relationship involved in the production process, and finally for the economy as a whole.

I

For a single straightforward exchange, I use the transfer of a residential property in the modern United States. This transfer involves a bundle of rights over a physical asset in exchange for a sum of money. The rights are both legal rights defining what one can do with the property and rights over the physical attributes of the property. The sum of money is a command over resources. Institutions determine how costly it is to make the exchange. The costs consist of the resources necessary to measure both the legal and physical attributes being exchanged, the costs of policing and enforcing the agreement, and an uncertainty discount reflecting the degree of imperfection in the measurement and enforcement of the terms of the exchange. The size of the uncertainty discount will be influenced by such specific-to-the-contract factors as asymmetric information about the condition of the house (known to the seller) and the financial condition of the buyer (known to the buyer), by such communitywide factors as the effectiveness of crime prevention, and by such nationwide factors as the stability of the price level.

In the seller's utility are the price, terms, and security of the contractual obligation, that is, the likelihood that the buyer will live up to the contract ex post. The value of the residence to the buyer is a function not only of price and credit terms but also of the attributes that are transferred with the sale. Some, such as the legal rights that are transferred and the dimensions of the property and house, are easily measured, and some, such as the general features of the property, are readily observed on inspection. But others, such as the maintenance and upkeep costs and the characteristics of neighbors, may be far more difficult to ascertain. Equally, the security of property against default, expropriation, uncertain title, and theft will vary according to the difficulty of ascertaining their likelihood and, therefore, their importance.

Now in the traditional neoclassical paradigm, with perfect information (i.e., zero transaction costs), the value of the asset that is transferred assumes not only perfect information but perfectly secure property rights as well. In that case, because both buyer and seller have been able to ascertain costlessly the value of all the attributes (both physical and property rights) and there is no uncertainty or insecurity of property rights, the standard supply and demand models of housing with zero transaction costs would define the value of the asset. In fact, because all of the above-mentioned attributes influence the value of the residence to the buyer and seller, the smaller the discount from the idealized neoclassical model, the more perfect the market. Institutions in the aggregate define and determine the size of the discount, and the transaction costs that the buyer and seller incur reflect the institutional framework.

The transaction costs of the transfer are partly market costs – such as legal fees, realtor fees, title insurance, and credit rating searches – and partly the costs of time each party must devote to gathering information, to searching, and so forth. Obtaining information about crime rates, police protection, and security systems entails search costs to the buyer.

Transaction and transformation costs

To the degree that the buyer's utility function is adversely affected by noisy neighbors or pets, it will pay to invest in ascertaining neighborhood characteristics and the norms and conventions that shape neighborhood interactions.

The particular institutions matrix of this housing market consists first of all of a hierarchy of legal rules derived from provisions of the U.S. constitution and the powers delegated to the states. State laws defining the conveyance characteristics of real property, zoning laws restricting which rights can be transferred, common and statute law undergirding, defining, or restricting a host of voluntary organizations – all of these influence transaction costs. Realtors, title insurance, credit bureaus, and savings and loan associations that affect the mortgage market all will be influenced. The efficiency of these organizations is a function of the structure of property rights and enforcement and of the capital market (including voluntary as well as governmental guarantees and subsidies and other instruments that exist in the capital market). Equally important are informal constraints that broadly supplement and reinforce the formal rules. They range from conventions of neighborhood conduct to ethical norms defining degrees of honesty in information exchange between the parties involved.

My description has emphasized institutions that lower transaction costs, but some – such as rules that restrict entry, require useless inspections, raise information costs, or make property rights less secure – in fact raise transaction costs. The above-mentioned economic rules are made in the polity and reflect the bargaining strength of contractors, trade unions, and others in the political market. Because that market is *imperfect,* institutions everywhere are a mixed bag composed of those that lower costs and those that raise them. The U.S. residential housing market is a relatively efficient market in which on balance the institutions induce low-cost transacting.

Returning to the model in Chapter 4, the discount from the frictionless exchange envisioned in economic theory will be greater to the degree that the institutional structure allows third parties to influence the value of attributes that are in the utility function of the buyer. These could include the behavior of neighbors, the likelihood of theft, and the possibility of changes by local authorities in zoning ordinances that may affect the value of the property. The greater the uncertainty of the buyer, the lower the value of the asset. Likewise, the institutional structure will determine the risks to the seller that the contract will be fulfilled or that the seller will be indemnified in case of default. It is worth emphasizing that the uncertainties described above with respect to the security of rights are a critical distinction between the relatively efficient markets of high income countries today and economies in the past as well as those in the Third World today.

II

Let us turn from examining the relationship between institutions and transactions costs in a straightforward exchange, and examine those involved in the productions of goods and services. The institutional framework will affect both transformation and transaction costs; the latter because of the direct connection between institutions and transaction costs, and the former by influencing the technology employed. All the usual problems of measurement and enforcement described in the previous section obtain: the structure of property rights, the effectiveness of the courts and judicial system, and the complementary development of voluntary organizations and norms. Specifically, the firm's entrepreneur must be able to ascertain the quantity and quality of a firm's inputs and outputs. Because these can be obtained costlessly in the neoclassical model, the contrast between a hypothetical neoclassical firm and a real firm is striking. The former was little more than a production function without any costs of organization, supervision, coordination, monitoring, and metering. A real-life firm must purchase inputs that constantly require measurement and metering if it is to produce outputs of constant quality. Variability in quality will, ceteris paribus, adversely affect demand for its products. When there is variability, consumers (or if this is an intermediate good, producers) must devote resources to ascertaining quality; hence producers who can guarantee constant quality will be favored.[1]

Perfect measurement and enforcement are implicitly assumed in what we call efficient factor and product markets, but their existence entails a complex set of institutions that encourage factor mobility, the acquisition of skills, uninterrupted production, rapid and low-cost transmission of information, and the invention and innovation of new technologies. Realizing all these conditions is a tall order never completely filled because, as with the institutions of exchange described above, the actual institutional framework is in fact usually a mixed bag of institutions that promote such productivity-raising activities and institutions that provide barriers to entry, encourage monopolistic restrictions, and impede the low-cost flow of information.

We have only to contrast the organization of production in a Third World economy with that in an advanced industrial economy to be im-

---

[1]For a fascinating analysis of the significant resource costs the producer must engage in to assure constant quality, see the detailed description of the production of peas in Susan Sheehan's essay "Peas," in *The New Yorker,* June 17, 1973. The trouble that Green Giant went to in attempting to ascertain size, tenderness, and sweetness in the production of peas involved enormous monitoring and metering resources that began in the field and did not end until the cans went off to the retailer.

pressed by the consequences of poorly defined and/or ineffective property rights. Not only will the institutional framework result in high costs of transacting in the former, but insecure property rights will result in using technologies that employ little fixed capital and do not entail long-term agreements. Firms will typically be small (except those operated or protected by the government). Moreover, such mundane problems as an inability to get spare parts or a two-year wait to get a telephone installed will necessitate a different organization of production than an advanced country requires. A bribe sufficient to get quick delivery through the maze of import controls or get rapid telephone installation may exist; but the resultant shadow transaction costs significantly alter relative prices and consequently the technology employed.

Even with the relatively secure property rights that exist in high-income countries, it is possible and indeed frequently the case that a technical combination that involves costly monitoring may be less efficient than a technique that has lower physical output but less variance in the product or lower costs of monitoring workers. Much of the recent transaction cost literature implies that institutions only determine transaction costs and techniques only determine transformation costs, but three different illustrations arising from the interplay between techniques, institutions, transformation costs, and transaction costs make clear that the relationship among them is more complex.

1. A contention of Marxist writers is that deliberate deskilling of the labor force occurred during the early twentieth century. That is, employers adopted capital-intensive technologies that eliminated highly skilled workers and replaced them with semiskilled or unskilled workers. The logic of this charge is that the bargaining power of skilled workers enabled them to disrupt the production process strategically, which, given the "high speed throughput" (Chandler's term) of modern technology was enormously costly. Employers found it reduced total cost over time to introduce technologies that used less-skilled workers who did not have the bargaining power to disrupt production. In this case, a new production technology was introduced to reduce transaction costs.

2. Unitizing an oil field, that is, creating an organization with the coercive power and monitoring authority to allocate the output of an oil field, raised transaction costs (because of the resources devoted to creating and maintaining an organization and then to monitoring compliance). At the same time, unitizing the field reduced transformation costs (the result of more efficient pumping and recovery) to an extent that more than offset the rise in transaction costs (Libecap and Wiggins, 1985). In this case an institutional change raised transaction costs that were more than compensated by lower transformation costs.

3. Andrea Shepard (1987) describes the deliberate policy of a semicon-

ductor manufacturer who licenses the designs of new chips to competitors, so that customers can be assured that the chip manufacturer will not be able to hold up customers who adopt the new design. By alleviating customers' concerns, it enhances demand for the product. Although this policy lowers transaction costs, it does so at the sacrifice of productive efficiency, because both scale economies and learning curve effects are lost to competing firms. Second sourcing appears to be a common practice.

Informal constraints frequently play a major role with respect to the quantity and quality of labor output. Although Marxists long ago recognized the key distinction between the quantity of labor input and the quantity and quality of output, it has only recently become a major focus of economists' attention (at least partially a consequence, in recent years, of the quality differences in labor output between Japanese and American automobile manufacturers). Conventions about output, forms of organization designed to encourage work participation and cooperation, and attempts to select workers who have an ideological commitment to hard work have all become recent research agendas in the New Industrial Organization. The unique feature of labor markets is that institutions are devised to take into account that the quantity and quality of output are influenced by the attitude of the productive factor – hence morale building is a substitute at the margin for investing in more monitoring.

III

Throughout the discussion above, it was emphasized that the cost of transacting reflects the overall complex of institutions – formal and informal – that make up an economy or, on an even greater scale, a society. This overall structure ultimately shapes the cost of transacting at the individual contract level, and when economists talk about efficient markets, they have simply taken for granted an elaborate framework of constraints. The cost of capital, for example, was in part determined by an elaborate structure of financial intermediaries whose interconnections among consumer credit and mortgage markets, stock markets, and bond markets were constrained by a complex structure of governmental constraints and regulatory agencies, from (in the United States) the Federal Reserve System to state laws and regulatory agencies dealing with everything from branch banking to interest rate ceilings. Moreover, behind the supply of and demand for capital are still other institutions and organizations such as title insurance and credit rating bureaus. Probing still more deeply into the institutional structure reveals political institutions that define formal constraints. The interconnection between the political and economic institutions and organizations is apparent in congressional committees that are concerned with the capital market and a host of lobbying organizations reflecting interested (and organized) groups in the capital market. The web of interconnections extends to the executive branch as well as to specific regulatory agencies. All of this, of course, has been grist for the new political economy in its attempt to spell out and provide an analytical framework for the institutional structures of Congress and other branches of government.

When we compare the cost of transacting in a Third World country with that in an advanced industrial economy, the costs per exchange in the former are much greater – sometimes no exchange occurs because costs are so high. The institutional structure in the Third World lacks the formal structure (and enforcement) that underpins efficient markets. However, frequently there will exist in Third World countries informal sectors (in effect underground economies) that attempt to provide a structure for exchange. Such structure comes at high costs, however, because the lack of formal property right safeguards restricts activity to personalized exchange systems that can provide self-enforcing types of contracts.[2] But there is more to the issue than simply higher transaction costs in Third World countries. In addition, the institutional framework, which determines the basic structure of production, tends to perpetuate underdevelopment.

Firms come into existence to take advantage of profitable opportunities, which will be defined by the existing set of constraints. With insecure property rights, poorly enforced laws, barriers to entry, and monopolistic restrictions, the profit-maximizing firms will tend to have short time horizons and little fixed capital, and will tend to be small scale. The most profitable businesses may be in trade, redistributive activities, or the black market. Large firms with substantial fixed capital will exist only under the umbrella of government protection with subsidies, tariff protection, and payoffs to the polity – a mixture hardly conducive to productive efficiency.

IV

I conclude this chapter by drawing out some of the implications of the foregoing analysis.

1. The institutional constraints that define the opportunity set of individuals are a complex of formal and informal constraints. They make up an interconnected web that in various combinations shapes choice sets in various contexts. It is easy, given this understanding, to see why institu-

[2]See Hernando de Soto's *The Other Path* (1989) for an insightful analysis of the structure of the Peruvian economy and the characteristics of the large informal sector.

tions are stable and why they typically produce many different margins at which choices are made.

Stability derives from the fact that there are a large number of specific constraints that affect a particular choice, such as those described in the sale of residential property. Significant changes in this institutional framework involve a host of changes in a variety of constraints, not only legal constraints but norms of behavior as well. Although the institutional constraints may not be ideal or efficient for one set of individuals involved in a particular exchange and therefore those parties would like to restructure the institutions, the same set of institutions for other sets of choices may still reflect as efficient a bargain as is possible. Moreover it is the bargaining strength of the individuals and organizations that counts. Hence, only when it is in the interest of those with sufficient bargaining strength to alter the formal rules will there be major changes in the formal institutional framework.

At the same time, the complex of informal and formal constraints makes possible continual incremental changes at particular margins. These small changes in both formal rules and informal constraints will gradually alter the institutional framework over time, so that it evolves into a different set of choices than it began with. Both the stability characteristics of institutions and the marginal incremental changes briefly discussed here will be the subject of Part II.

2. The complex of institutional constraints will result in various mixes of formal and informal constraints, which in turn reflect the costliness of measurement and enforcement. The higher these costs, the more will the exchanging parties invoke informal constraints to shape the exchange, although in the extreme, of course, no exchange will take place at all. Vertical integration offers a partial solution to these costs, always with the caveat that although measurement costs inside organizations will differ from those across markets, they are not necessarily lower. To the extent that informal constraints will dominate forms of exchange, they will typically take the form of devising ways to get around the likelihood of defection by the other party. Therefore self-enforcing contracts, such as those described in Chapter 7, will dominate forms of exchange, although there is the recognition of the limitations that necessarily obtain when third-party enforcement is not possible.

3. Transaction costs are the most observable dimension of the institutional framework that underlies the constraints in exchange. They consist of those costs that go through the market (see Wallis and North, 1986) and therefore are measurable, and of hard-to-measure costs that include time acquiring information, queuing, bribery, and so forth, as well as the losses due to imperfect monitoring and enforcement. These hard-to-measure costs make it difficult to assess precisely the total transaction costs

resulting from a particular institution. Nevertheless, to the degree we are able to do so, we progress in measuring the effectiveness of institutions.

The level of interest rates in capital markets is perhaps the most evident quantitative dimension of the efficiency of the institutional framework, but in Third World countries telephone systems that do not work, the inability to get spare parts, endless production interruptions, long queues and waiting time to get permits, and product variability are overwhelming evidence that an effective institutional infrastructure does not exist.

4. The most important moral to be drawn from this chapter is that the institutional framework plays a major role in the performance of an economy. The sale of the house described earlier in this chapter illustrates what is at stake. A large number of institutions makes possible a mass market in housing and the capital market, the institutions that made for security of property rights, and the large number of voluntary organizations that facilitate the exchange play key roles in the existence of the relatively efficient residential market in the United States as compared to similar housing markets in Third World countries or, in the distant past, in the United States. However, I have been at pains to point out that some institutional constraints raise transaction costs. Therefore, the market overall is a mixed bag of institutions; some increase efficiency and some decrease efficiency. Nevertheless, contrasting the institutional framework in countries such as the United States, England, France, Germany, and Japan with Third World countries or those in the historical past in advanced industrial countries makes clear that this institutional framework is the critical key to the relative success of economies, both cross-sectionally as well as through time. The way institutional constraints evolve through time and thereby determine the performance characteristics of economies is the focus of the rest of this book.

Part II

Institutional change

9

Organizations, learning, and institutional change

In Chapter 8, I moved from institutions and transaction costs to aspects of an economy's performance, excluding organizations from my analysis. In Chapter 1 I introduced the relationship between institutions and organizations, and I now return to it. Organizations and their entrepreneurs engage in purposive activity and in that role are the agents of, and shape the direction of, institutional change. I propose in this chapter to show how organizations induce change.

I begin by returning to the Coase (1937) argument that transaction costs are the basis for the existence of the firm. If information and enforcement were costless, it would be hard to envision a significant role for organizations. But they are not. What is the role of organization? The firm, a form of organization, has been considered a device to exploit the worker (Marglin, 1974), to overcome the problems of asset specificity and postcontractual opportunism (Williamson, 1975, 1985), and to reduce measurement costs in economic activity (Barzel, 1982).

Whatever the merits of these alternatives (and they are not altogether mutually exclusive), the focus in this study is on organizations as purposive entities designed by their creators to maximize wealth, income, or other objectives defined by the opportunities afforded by the institutional structure of the society.

In the course of pursuing those objectives, organizations incrementally alter the institutional structure. They are not, however, necessarily socially productive because the institutional framework frequently has perverse incentives. Organizations will be designed to further the objectives of their creators. They will be created as a function not simply of institutional constraints but also of other constraints (e.g., technology, income, and preferences). The interaction of these constraints shapes the potential wealth-maximizing opportunities of entrepreneurs (economic or political). If we wish to explore the existence of guilds or the manor in medieval Europe, the regulated company in early modern Europe, the estates gener-

73

al in fifteenth-century France, or the committee structure of Congress, the Mafia, or General Motors in twentieth-century United States, our models must not only take into account literature that has recently evolved on the firm and the polity, but also integrate into the analysis the way institutional constraints have shaped these organizations and their objectives. The kinds of knowledge and skills that will be acquired by the organization to further its objectives will in turn play a major role in the way the stock of knowledge evolves and is used.

I

Using the competitive team sports analogy, given a set of formal and informal rules and enforcement characteristics that broadly define the way the game is played, what can we say about the play that we observe? Obviously, a critical factor is the skill of the players and the knowledge they possess of the game. Even with a constant set of rules, the games played will differ if they are played between rank amateurs and professionals or between a team in its first game and the same team in its one hundredth game together. The contrasts come from the differences between communicable knowledge and tacit knowledge in the case of amateurs and professionals and from learning by doing in the case of repeated team play.

Communicable knowledge is, as the name implies, knowledge that can be transmitted from one person to another. Tacit knowledge (a term coined by Michael Polanyi, 1967) is acquired in part by practice and can be only partially communicated; different individuals have different innate abilities for acquiring tacit knowledge. One cannot learn to play a good game of tennis solely from a book, and even with practice there is an immense difference between players. What holds for any sport also applies to a great many kinds of skills, of which entrepreneurial skill is perhaps the most important. Learning by doing in organizations, as the term implies, means that an organization acquires coordination skills and develops routines that work as a consequence of repeated interaction (Nelson and Winter, 1982, explore these issues).

The kinds of knowledge, skills, and learning that the members of an organization will acquire will reflect the payoff – the incentives – imbedded in the institutional constraints. The Mafia will develop different skills than will General Motors executives, or to take a more prosaic example from economic history, the skills and knowledge essential to the Merchant Adventurers (wool cloth exporters in the fifteenth century) were very different than those essential to the success of a modern textile-exporting firm. Self-evident as this point may be, it has profound implications for institutional change. The demand for knowledge and skills will in turn create a demand for increases in the stock and distribution of knowledge, and the nature of that demand will reflect current perceptions about the payoffs to acquiring different kinds of knowledge. Thus, the demand for investment in knowledge is radically different today in the United States than in Iran or, to go back to history, Europe in the Middle Ages. The rate of return (private) to increases in knowledge may reflect high returns to improvements in military technology (in medieval Europe), to the pursuit and refinement of religious dogma (Rome during and after Constantine), or more prosaically to the search for an accurate chronometer (to enable mariners to determine longitude at sea and for which large rewards were offered during the age of exploration).

The incentives to acquire pure knowledge are affected not only by the structure of monetary rewards and punishments, but also by a society's tolerance of its development, as a long list of creative individuals from Galileo to Darwin could attest to. The literature dealing with the origins and development of science is substantial, but I am not aware that much of it self-consciously explores the connecting links between institutional structures as defined in this study and incentives to acquire pure knowledge. However, a major factor in the development of Western Europe was the gradual perception of the utility of research in pure science.

The conversion of pure to applied knowledge has been the subject of much more direct scholarly attention, and the literature devoted to technological change, from Schumpeter and Schmookler to David and Rosenberg, is substantial. With respect to this literature, four points should be emphasized.

1. In the absence of property rights incentives, the size of the market was the most important single determinant of the rate of growth of innovation and technological change (Sokoloff, 1988).
2. The development of an incentive structure through patent laws, trade secret laws, and other laws raised the rate of return on innovation and also led to the development of the invention industry and its integration into the way economies evolved in the Western world in modern times, which in turn underlay the Second Economic Revolution.[1]
3. The relationship between pure and applied knowledge is not a simple one, as Rosenberg (1976) has pointed out. Pure knowledge is a prerequisite of applied knowledge, but developments of applied knowledge have opened up and suggested issues that should be explored. Thus

[1]However, see the most recent work of Richard Nelson, entitled "Capitalism as an Engine of Progress," forthcoming, in which the author explores the various ways that firms attempt to capture the gains from innovation and finds out that while patenting is important in some kinds of industries, secrets and other devices become more and more important as the process of innovating becomes more complex.

applied knowledge has been a major source of the growth of pure knowledge.

4. The development of technology illuminates the path-dependent character of the way in which technologies change. This point has important implications for the rest of this study. Once technology develops along a particular path, given increasing returns, alternative paths and alternative technologies may be shunted aside and ignored, hence development may be entirely led down a particular path. The results are not always optimal downstream, as Arthur (1989) and David (1985) have demonstrated.

The distribution of knowledge has also been the subject of a recent large literature involved most typically with a discussion of human capital, which in turn is largely a function of the development of schooling and on-the-job training. Because the development of schooling has been, at least in large part, a function of the institutional characteristics of a society, it is a dependent variable in this analysis. The critical point is that investments in human and physical capital tend to be complementary and, given imperfections in the human capital market, there are no guarantees that the growth of human capital will keep pace with the growth of the physical capital structure.

On the subject of knowledge and ideology, there is much less literature and all too little is known. But let me emphasize that it is a two-way relationship, that is, the way knowledge develops shapes our perceptions of the world around us and in turn those perceptions shape the search for knowledge. Clearly, intellectual life during the Middle Ages in the West was dominated, with respect to learning, by the church, and even today ideologies in many parts of the world are intolerant, to one degree or another, of the development of pure knowledge. The way in which knowledge develops influences the perceptions people have about the world around them and hence the way in which they rationalize, explain, and justify that world, which in turn influences the costs of contracting. People's perceptions that the structure of rules of the system is fair and just reduce costs; equally, their perception that the system is unjust raises the costs of contracting (given the costliness of measurement and enforcement of contracts).

II

I will integrate the maximizing objectives of the organization, which have been conditioned by the institutional framework, with the development of the stock of knowledge. If we start with the neoclassical firm, the only function of management is to select profit-maximizing quantities of outputs and inputs, which means determining the quantity and the consequent price that will be established. Because information for doing this is also freely at hand and the calculations are costless, the model strips from management any meaningful productivity in the performance of even those tasks. There are no costs, in short, to maximization.

This neoclassical approach came under critical evaluation, first in Knight's *Risk, Uncertainty and Profit* (1921) and then in Coase's "The Nature of the Firm" (1937), both of which began to redirect the attention of economists looking at organization. Knight focused on the role of the entrepreneur in attempting to reduce uncertainty, and Coase introduced the concept of transaction costs, which began to make sense of the existence of the firm. In fact, the real tasks of management are to devise and discover markets, to evaluate products and product techniques, and to manage actively the actions of employees; these are all tasks in which there is uncertainty and in which investment in information must be acquired.[2]

Discovering markets, evaluating markets and techniques, and managing employees do not occur in a vacuum. They entail the development of tacit knowledge to unravel the complexities associated with problems of measurement and enforcement. The kinds of information and knowledge required by the entrepreneur are in good part a consequence of a particular institutional context. That context will not only shape the internal organization and determine the extent of vertical integration and governance structure, but also determine the pliable margins that offer the greatest promise in maximizing the organization's objectives. Therefore, we need to examine the institutional context to see what kind of demand exists for different kinds of knowledge and skills.

To be a successful pirate one needs to know a great deal about naval warfare; the trade routes of commercial shipping; the armament, rigging, and crew size of the potential victims; and the market for booty. Successful pirates will acquire the requisite knowledge and skills. Such activities may well give rise to a thriving demand for improved naval warfare technology by both the pirates and the victims.

To be a successful chemical manufacturer in early twentieth-century United States required knowledge of chemistry, potental uses of chemicals in different intermediate and final products, markets, and problems of large-scale organization. Successful chemical manufacturers gave rise to a demand for both applied and pure chemical research as well as the study of markets and new forms of organization to reduce production and transaction costs.

[2]For an excellent analysis of the theory of the firm developed along these lines, see Harold Demsetz, "The Theory of the Firm Revisited" (1988).

Institutional change

If the basic institutional framework makes income redistribution (piracy) the preferred (most profitable) economic opportunity, we can expect a very different development of knowledge and skills than a productivity-increasing (the twentieth-century chemical manufacturer) economic opportunity would entail. Extreme examples, yes, but as ideal types they do typify much of economic history. The incentives that are built into the institutional framework play the decisive role in shaping the kinds of skills and knowledge that pay off.

I am not implying that there is a simplistic relationship that unambiguously predicts the downstream consequences; the maximizing efforts of entrepreneurs frequently have unanticipated consequences (Chapter 10). For example, the research in naval warfare could result in techniques that would eradicate piracy, and the organizational research of my twentieth-century firm could lead to the discovery of a new legal way of cartelizing the chemical industry. But the general points I wish to make here are, I believe, quite clear: (1) the institutional framework will shape the direction of the acquisition of knowledge and skills and (2) that direction will be the decisive factor for the long-run development of that society. If the firm or other economic organization invests in knowledge that increases the productivity of the physical or human capital inputs or improves the tacit knowledge of the entrepreneurs, then the resultant productivity increase is also consistent with the growth of the economy. But what if maximizing behavior by the firm consists of burning down or sabotaging competitors, or of labor organizations engaging in slowdowns or makework, or of farmers getting the government to restrict farm output and raise prices? The institutional framework dictates the maximizing opportunities for the organization and even in the most productive economies in the modern world the signals generated by the institutional framework are mixed, as is shown in even the most casual scrutiny of the formal rules and enforcement characteristics of the present U.S. economy. We have institutions that reward restrictions on output, makework, and crime, just as we have institutions that reward productive economic activity. On balance, the latter have outweighed the former, but they have not done so through most of human history nor do they in many Third World economies today.

Maximizing behavior of economic organizations therefore shapes institutional change by: (1) the resultant derived demand for investment in knowledge of all kinds (discussed above); (2) the ongoing interaction between organized economic activity, the stock of knowledge, and the institutional framework (discussed below); and (3) incremental alteration of the informal constraints as a by-product of maximizing activities of organizations (discussed in Chapter 10).

III

Maximizing behavior by the firm can take the form of making choices within the existing set of constraints or of altering the constraints. The modern literature on the firm by Williamson and others explores the most efficient governance structure and organization within the existing institutional constraints.[3] Such maximizing activity by the firm results from learning by doing and investing in the kinds of skills and knowledge that will pay off. But an alternative is to devote resources to changing the institutional constraints. Which direction the firm or economic organization takes depends upon its subjective perception of the payoffs. Clearly, in the modern U.S. economy, economic organizations devote resources to both. What determines the relative payoffs and the kind of institutional change that organizations will attempt to achieve through political activity?

In Chapter 6 I developed a transaction cost model of the polity and briefly explored the interaction of the economy and the polity. Here I wish to focus on the incremental process of change that will result from this interaction. Organizations with sufficient bargaining strength will use the polity to achieve objectives when the payoff from maximizing in that direction exceeds the payoff from investing within the existing constraints. But the incremental change in the overall institutional framework is more comprehensive than what happens when economic organizations devote resources to changing political rules directly to increase their profitability. Organizations will also encourage the society to invest in the kinds of skills and knowledge that indirectly contribute to their profitability. Such investment will shape the long-run growth of skills and knowledge, which are the underlying determinants of economic growth.

U.S. economic history is illustrative. The perceived rewards to increased knowledge and education in the nineteenth century induced public and private investment in formal education, on-the-job training, and applied research both in agricultural and industrial activities. The result was not only the gradual transformation of economic organizations as described by Chandler (1977) and the growth of educational organizations with their own agendas and influence on the polity, but also the evolving perceptions of politicians and voters of the value of such investment. The results were certainly not unidirectional. Darwinian theory ran afoul of creationist arguments, and the tension between religious orthodoxy and scientific developments persists to today. The overall result has, however,

---

[3]See Williamson's *The Economic Institutions of Capitalism* (1985) for an insightful exploration of these issues.

reinforced the initial perception of the complementarity between economic performance and investment in the growth and dissemination of knowledge. The United States has been immensely productive in the twentieth century. The significant implication of this story is that the market for knowledge together with the subjective perceptions of the players coincided to produce a private and public investment in knowledge that approached the social rate of return.

Throughout most history the institutional incentives to invest in productive knowledge have been largely absent, and even in Third World economies today the incentives are frequently misdirected. If Third World countries do invest in education, they frequently misdirect the investment into higher education, not primary education (which has a much higher social rate of return than does higher education in Third World countries). Why is there such a contrast with the U.S. story? If the private market had been efficient, then the correct investment would have occurred through voluntary organizations. But if that market was imperfect so that the private rates of return were so low as not to make such private investment worthwhile, then the correct investment (in primary education) could have been undertaken by public investment, assuming members of the society appreciated that there was a high social rate of return on such investment. But the fact that such public investment was not undertaken or was misdirected suggests not only high transaction costs resulting in imperfect markets, but also that imperfect knowledge and understanding make up the subjective models of the actors.

IV

I want to draw out some of the implications of the interaction of purposive organizations (and their entrepreneurs) and institutions for the performance of economies over time. The systematic investment in skills and knowledge and their application to an economy suggests a dynamic evolution of that economy that entails a specific set of institutional characteristics. A description of these characteristics requires us to think of the issues of efficiency in a context different than straightforward allocative efficiency. In allocative efficiency, the standard neoclassical Pareto conditions obtain. Adaptive efficiency, on the other hand, is concerned with the kinds of rules that shape the way an economy evolves through time.[4] It is also concerned with the willingness of a society to acquire knowledge and learning, to induce innovation, to undertake risk and creative activity of all sorts, as well as to resolve problems and bottlenecks of the society through time.

[4]See Pavel Pelikan (1987) for an elaboration of this argument.

Organizations, learning, and change

We are far from knowing all the aspects of what makes for adaptive efficiency, but clearly the overall institutional structure plays the key role in the degree that the society and the economy will encourage the trials, experiments, and innovations that we can characterize as adaptively efficient. The incentives embedded in the institutional framework direct the process of learning by doing and the development of tacit knowledge that will lead individuals in decision-making processes to evolve systems gradually that are different from the ones that they had to begin with. We need only to read, again, Armen Alchian (1950) to understand this. In a world of uncertainty, no one knows the correct answer to the problems we confront and no one therefore can, in effect, maximize profits. The society that permits the maximum generation of trials will be most likely to solve problems through time (a familiar argument of Hayek, 1960). Adaptive efficiency, therefore, provides the incentives to encourage the development of decentralized decision-making processes that will allow societies to maximize the efforts required to explore alternative ways of solving problems. We must also learn from failures, so that change will consist of the generation of organizational trials and the elimination of organizational errors. There is nothing simple about this process, because organizational errors may be not only probabilistic, but also systematic, due to ideologies that may give people preferences for the kinds of solutions that are not oriented to adaptive efficiency.

Now, different institutional rules will produce different incentives for tacit knowledge. That is, the particular institution will not only determine the kinds of economic activity that will be profitable and viable, but also shape the adaptive efficiency of the internal structure of firms and other organizations by, for example, regulating entry, governance structures, and the flexibility of organizations. In particular, rules that encourage the development and utilization of tacit knowledge and therefore creative entrepreneurial talent will be important for efficient organization. The studies by Nelson and Winter (1982) and Pelikan (1987) are important contributions to the study of effective organization.

Obviously, competition, decentralized decision making, and well-specified contracts of property rights as well as bankruptcy laws are crucial to effective organization. It is essential to have rules that eliminate not only failed economic organization but failed political organization as well. The effective structure of rules, therefore, not only rewards successes, but also vetoes the survival of maladapted parts of the organizational structure, which means that effective rules will dissolve unsuccessful efforts as well as promote successful efforts.

We are far from understanding how to achieve adaptively efficient economies because allocative efficiency and adaptive efficiency may not always be consistent. Allocatively efficient rules would make today's firms and decisions secure – but frequently at the expense of the creative destruction process that Schumpeter had in mind. Moreover, the very nature of the political process encourages the growth of constraints that favor today's influential bargaining groups. But adaptively efficient institutional frameworks have existed and do exist, just as adaptively inefficient frameworks have existed and do exist.

10

Stability and institutional change

The agent of change is the individual entrepreneur responding to the incentives embodied in the institutional framework. The sources of change are changing relative prices or preferences. The process of change is overwhelmingly an incremental one. I will put those separate elements together in this chapter.

Change typically consists of marginal adjustments to the complex of rules, norms, and enforcement that constitute the institutional framework. The overall stability of an institutional framework makes complex exchange possible across both time and space, and it will be useful to review the stability characteristics to improve our understanding of the nature of the incremental process of change.

Stability is accomplished by a complex set of constraints that include formal rules nested in a hierarchy, where each level is more costly to change than the previous one. They also include informal constraints, which are extensions, elaborations, and qualifications of rules and have tenacious survival ability because they have become part of habitual behavior. They allow people to go about the everyday process of making exchanges without having to think out exactly the terms of an exchange at each point and in each instance. Routines, customs, traditions, and conventions are words we use to note the persistence of informal constraints, and it is the complex interaction of formal rules and informal constraints, together with the way they are enforced, that shapes our daily living and directs us in the mundane (the very word conjures up images of institutional stability) activities that dominate our lives. Although the mix of rules and norms varies, as I have discussed, the combination nevertheless provides us with the comfortable feeling of knowing what we are doing and where we are going.

It is important to stress once more, however, that this set of stability features in no way guarantees that the institutions relied upon are efficient (in the sense that the term is used in this study), although stability may be a necessary condition for complex human interaction, it is certainly not a sufficient condition for efficiency.

I

Institutions change, and fundamental changes in relative prices are the most important source of that change. To the noneconomist (and perhaps for some economists as well), putting such weight on changing relative prices may be hard to understand. But relative price changes alter the incentives of individuals in human interaction, and the only other source of such change is a change in tastes.

All of the following sources of institutional changes are changes in relative prices: changes in the ratio of factor prices (i.e., changes in the ratio of land to labor, labor to capital, or capital to land), changes in the cost of information, and changes in technology (including significantly and importantly, military technology). Some of these relative price changes will be exogenous to the analytical framework advanced in the previous chapter (such as the changes in land/labor ratios that resulted from the plague in late medieval Europe); but most will be endogenous, reflecting the ongoing maximizing efforts of entrepreneurs (political, economic, and military) that will alter relative prices and in consequence induce institutional change. The process by which the entrepreneur acquires skills and knowledge is going to change relative prices by changing perceived costs of measurement and enforcement and by altering perceived costs and benefits of new bargains and contracts.

Changes in bargaining power lead to efforts to restructure contracts, political as well as economic. Because in previous studies (North and Thomas, 1973; North, 1981) I have dealt with the role changing relative prices play, I shall not go into the subject further here. Rather, I would like to explore the much more troublesome and more difficult problem of changes in tastes.

We know very little about the sources of changing preferences or tastes. It is clear that changing relative prices play some role in changes in taste. That is, fundamental changes in relative prices over time will alter the behavioral pattern of people and their rationalization of what constitutes standards of behavior. I choose a modern example. The changing structure of the family in the twentieth century has been fundamentally shaped by changing relative prices of work, leisure, and contraception. Well-known studies by Fuchs (1983) and Becker (1981) document in great detail the ways by which family structure has changed in this century. Accompanying change in family structures has been a change in ideological attitudes to moral issues and to the role of women in society. To account for the complex changes in norms of behavior of modern Western women in terms of relative price changes alone, however, is a vast over-simplification of a complex and still little understood aspect of human behavior. Changing relative prices are filtered through preexisting mental constructs that shape our understanding of those price changes. Clearly ideas, and the way they take hold, play a role here. The exact mix of the two – price changes and ideas – is still far from clear.

I elaborate further using another classic case. A major institutional change that by itself cannot be entirely accounted for by a change in relative prices and in which ideas mattered was the consequence of the growing abhorrence on the part of civilized human beings of one person owning another and therefore the rise of the antislavery movement throughout the world. Clearly, as we have learned in the tremendous scholarly controversy over the nature of slavery in the United States, this institution was still profitable at the time of the Civil War. Of course, the antislavery movement had long roots and was a complex story, and it was used by some groups for their own interests. For example, the slavery issue was used to change relative bargaining strengths in regional conflicts between the North and the South over changing relations with the West in issues of political control of the U.S. Congress in the first half of the nineteenth century. But it was the intellectual power of the antislavery movement per se that enabled politicians to exploit the issue (Fogel, 1989). What perhaps needs stressing more than anything else is that individuals could express their abhorrence of slavery at relatively little cost to themselves and at the same time exact a very high price from slave owners. The point I am making reinforces the argument advanced in earlier chapters that the structure of institutions, in this case the electoral process, makes it possible for people to express their ideas and ideologies effectively at very little cost to themselves. Thus, in Britain in the 1830s, as in the United States in 1860, voters did just that on the slavery issue (although in British possessions slave owners were compensated and in the United States the outcome might have been very different had the North foreseen the price it would pay in the Civil War). The key here is that there was no method in the institutional structure by which the Southern slave owners could somehow bribe or pay off the voters to prevent them from voicing their beliefs.

The brief analysis of the elimination of slavery is built upon an institutional structure that allows people to express their views at little cost to themselves. I do not mean to imply that there are not occasions in which people are willing to engage in substantial sacrifices for their ideas and ideals; indeed, the degree to which people feel strongly about their ideological views may frequently lead them to engage in very substantial sacrifices, and such sacrifices have played a major role throughout history. But a major point of this study is that institutions, by reducing the price we pay for our convictions, make ideas, dogmas, fads, and ideologies important sources of institutional change. In turn, improved understanding of institutional change requires greater understanding than we now possess of just what makes ideas and ideologies catch hold. Therefore, we are still at something of a loss to define, in very precise terms, the interplay between changes in relative prices, the ideas and ideologies that form people's perceptions, and the roles that the two play in inducing changes in institutions.

II

Organizations are continually evolving and prices are changing all the time. When do relative price changes lead to institutional change and when are they simply a source of recontracting within the framework of the existing rules? The easiest way to think of these issues is in an equilibrium context. Institutional equilibrium would be a situation where given the bargaining strength of the players and the set of contractual bargains that made up total economic exchange, none of the players would find it advantageous to devote resources into restructuring the agreements. Note that such a situation does not imply that everyone is happy with the existing rules and contracts, but only that the relative costs and benefits of altering the game among the contracting parties does not make it worthwhile to do so. The existing institutional constraints defined and created the equilibrium.

The process of institutional change can be described as follows. A change in relative prices leads one or both parties to an exchange, whether it is political or economic, to perceive that either or both could do better with an altered agreement or contract. An attempt will be made to renegotiate the contract. However, because contracts are nested in a hierarchy of rules, the renegotiation may not be possible without restructuring a higher set of rules (or violating some norm of behavior). In that case, the party that stands to improve his or her bargaining position may very well attempt to devote resources to restructuring the rules at a higher level. In the case of a norm of behavior, a change in relative prices or a change in tastes will lead to its gradual erosion and to its replacement by a different norm. Over time, the rule may be changed or simply be ignored and unenforced. Similarly, a custom or tradition may be gradually eroded and replaced with another. This very simplified story can be complicated in many ways – by agenda power, by the free-rider problem, or by the tenacity of norms of behavior. But as the skeletal outline of the pattern of institutional change, it provides some basic characteristics.

Missing from the outline sketched here is the chief actor. Although changes in informal constraints – norms of behavior – may very well

evolve without any specific purposive activity by individuals or organizations, changes in formal rules and/or enforcement will usually require
substantial resources or at the very least overcoming the free-rider problem. As described above, entrepreneurs and their organizations will respond to changing (perceived) price ratios either directly, by devoting
resources to new profitable opportunities or – when change is unrealiza-
ble within existing rules – indirectly, by estimating the costs and benefits
of devoting resources to altering the rules or enforcement of rules.

The (political or economic) entrepreneurs may devote their talents or
tacit knowledge to ferreting out profitable margins, estimating the likelihood of success, and risking the organization's resources to capture
potential gains. Obviously, the efficiency of organizations depends on
perceiving and realizing those opportunities. To the degree that there are
large payoffs to influencing the rules and their enforcement, it will pay to
create intermediary organizations (trade associations, lobbying groups,
political action committees) between economic organizations and political bodies to realize the potential gains of political change. The larger the
percentage of society's resources influenced by government decisions (directly or via regulation), the more resources will be devoted to such
offensive and defensive (to prevent being adversely affected) organizations.

How do informal constraints change? Although we are not yet able to
explain precisely the forces that shape cultural evolution, it is obvious
that the cultural characteristics of a society change over time and that
accidents, learning, and natural selection all play a part (Boyd and Richerson, 1985). The most common explanations lean heavily upon evolutionary theory, although with the additional feature that acquired characteristics are culturally transmitted. However, cultural evolutionary theory
is in its infancy and is not of much immediate value in analyzing changing
specific informal constraints, except for one important point: the persistence of cultural traits in the face of changes in relative prices, formal
rules, or political status makes informal constraints change at a different
rate than formal rules.

If at the macrolevel of cultural inheritance we still know very little, we
can say more about changing informal constraints at a microlevel. In
part, as suggested above, changes in relative prices or tastes may result in
such constraints simply being ignored by common consent and then with-
ering away. In terms of the focus of this study, a major role of informal
constraints is to modify, supplement, or extend formal rules. Therefore, a
change in formal rules or their enforcement will result in a disequilibrium
situation, because what makes up a stable choice theoretic context is the
total package of formal and informal constraints and enforcement aspects. Note, however, that a change in either institutional constraint will

87

alter the transaction costs and give rise to efforts to evolve new conventions or norms that will effectively solve the new problems that will have arisen (Ellickson, forthcoming). A new informal equilibrium will evolve gradually after a change in the formal rules.[1] However, sometimes formal rules are developed deliberately to overrule and supersede existing informal constraints that no longer meet the needs of newly evolved bargaining structures. Usually, the norms (informal constraints) that have evolved to supplement formal rules persist in periods of stability, but get overturned by new formal rules in periods of change. Thus, the 1974 Bill of Rights of subcommittees in the House of Representatives in the United States produced a sharp change in formal rules that overrode previous informal committee structures. The change reflected a decline in party power over legislation and a sharp increase in the number of new liberal Democrats with a different agenda; in preceding committees that were primarily run by conservative Southern Democrats, their smaller number had made it impossible for them to realize their objectives (see Shepsle, 1989).

Changes in enforcement also provide organizational entrepreneurs with new avenues of profitable exploitation that in turn shift the direction of institutional change. The history of U.S. land law in the nineteenth century was a spectacular case in point. The mix of changing specific disposal rules (size, credit terms, price, and requirements) and profitable opportunities (resulting from changes in transportation, population, technology, and resources) and the small amount of resources the federal government devoted to enforcement (although that too varied) led to a vast array of individuals, groups, and organizations attempting to capture the benefits from exploiting land. Frequently, evading the law in the context of lax enforcement was a successful strategy. Land companies, squatters, claims clubs, lumber companies, railroad companies, mining companies, and cattlemen's associations all shaped U.S. land disposal and the consequent reactions of the federal government.[2] For example, after the Revolutionary War, squatters had traditionally settled on land and the states had granted them preemption rights. However, when the federal government took over land disposal in the 1790s, it did not follow suit but instead burned out squatters. An ongoing tug of war resulted and led to inconsistent policies, widespread evasion, and more than twenty acts by Congress between 1799 and 1830 that granted preemption rights to squatters in specific regions. Finally, a general preemption act was passed in 1830 and made permanent in 1841.[3]

[1]For political modeling of this process in Congress, see Shepsle and Weingast (1987).

[2]An old but still good summary of the very extensive literature is Carstensen (1963).
[3]See North and Rutten (1987).

III

Wars, revolutions, conquest, and natural disasters are sources of discontinuous institutional change and are the subject of the next section of this chapter. But the single most important point about institutional change, which must be grasped if we are to begin to get a handle on the subject, is that institutional change is overwhelmingly incremental. Thus, when we consider the demise of feudalism and manorialism, we observe that it consisted of a gradual restructuring of a framework in which the interconnections between formal and informal constraints and enforcement characteristics evolved over centuries. The agreement between lord and serf reflected the overwhelming power of the lord vis à vis the serf; but changes at the margin as a consequence of population decline in the fourteenth century altered the opportunity and increased the bargaining power of serfs, leading to the gradual demise of the traditional agreement between lord and serf, the emergence of copyhold, and eventually fee-simple ownership of land. The changes that altered the feudal structure were interwoven over a long period with changes at other margins (e.g., the technology of warfare). The customs of the manor were eroded and there were formal legal changes (such as the Statute of Wills). The important point is that the changes were an aggregation of literally thousands of specific small alterations in agreements between lords and serfs, which in total made for fundamental institutional change.

IV

By discontinuous change I mean a radical change in the formal rules, usually as a result of conquest or revolution. I do not provide a theory of revolution, which is the subject of an enormous literature,[4] but given the theoretical framework developed here, several observations are pertinent.[5]

1. Incremental change means that the parties to exchange recontract to capture some of the potential gains from trade (at least for one of the exchanging parties). Such recontracting can range from a very simple kind to what Skocpol calls political revolutions, in which a restructuring of political institutions resolves a gridlock crisis. The key to continuous incremental changes is institutional contexts that make possible new bargains and compromises between the players. Political institutions (both

---

[4]See Skocpol (1979) for a recent and thoughtful contribution.
[5]This argument will be elaborated, extended, and illustrated in a work in progress by Barry Weingast and myself.

formal and informal) can provide a hospitable framework for evolutionary change. If such an institutional framework has not evolved, the parties to an exchange may not have a framework to settle disputes, the potential gains from exchange cannot be realized, and entrepreneurs (as described in the previous chapter) may attempt to form a coalition of groups to break out of the deadlock by strikes, violence, and other means.

2. The inability to achieve compromise solutions may reflect not only a lack of mediating institutions, but also limited degrees of freedom of the entrepreneurs to bargain and still maintain the loyalty of their constituent groups. Thus, the real choice sets of the conflicting parties may have no intersection, so that even though there are potentially large gains from resolving the disagreements, the combination of the limited bargaining freedom of the entrepreneurs and a lack of facilitating institutions makes it impossible to do so.

3. Because neither party to a dispute is likely to have the muscle to win by itself, the parties must form coalitions and make deals with other interest groups. However, as a result the final outcomes of successful revolutions become very uncertain, because conflict within the coalition over the restructuring of the rules, and hence the distribution of rewards, leads to further conflict.

4. Broad based support for violent action requires ideological commitment to overcome the free-rider problem (North, 1981, Chapter 5). The stronger the ideological conviction of the participants, the greater the price they will be willing to pay and hence the more likely the revolution will be successful.

5. Such discontinuous change has some features in common with discontinuous evolutionary changes (characterized in demographic theory as punctuated equilibrium), but perhaps its most striking feature is that it is seldom as discontinuous as it appears on the surface (or in the utopian visions of revolutionaries). It is seldom so discontinuous partly because coalitions essential for the success of revolutions tend to have a short afterlife. The glue of ideological alienation and a common opponent is replaced by the dissolving solvents of ideological differences and conflicting payoff demands. One faction may simply eliminate the others, but more common is a lengthy period of uneasy and quarrelsome compromise.

Additionally, although ideological commitment is a necessary condition for mass support of a revolution, it is difficult to sustain. Giving up wealth and income for other values is one thing in the face of a common and hated oppressor, but the value of the trade-off changes as the oppressor disappears. Therefore, to the extent that the new formal rules are built on an incentive system that entails ideological commitment, they are going to be subverted and force reversion to more compatible constraints, as modern socialist economies have discovered.

Perhaps most important of all, the formal rules change, but the informal constraints do not. In consequence, there develops an ongoing tension between informal constraints and the new formal rules, as many are inconsistent with each other. The informal constraints had gradually evolved as extensions of previous formal rules. An immediate tendency, as has been described, is to have new formal rules supplant the persisting informal constraints. Such change is sometimes possible, in particular in a *partial equilibrium context,* but it ignores the deep-seated cultural inheritance that underlies many informal constraints. Although a wholesale change in the formal rules may take place, at the same time there will be many informal constraints that have great survival tenacity because they still resolve basic exchange problems among the participants, be they social, political, or economic. The result over time tends to be a restructuring of the overall constraints – in both directions – to produce a new equilibrium that is far less revolutionary.

11

The path of institutional change

I now turn to two fundamental questions of societal, political, and economic change. First, what determines the divergent patterns of evolution of societies, polities, or economies over time? And how do we account for the survival of economies with persistently poor performance over long periods of time?

If we look back far enough in history, divergence appears to be very simple to explain. Bands and tribes confronted different problems with different resource endowments, different human capabilities, and in different climates. Out of these emerged different solutions to the common problems of survival, including different languages, customs, traditions, and taboos. There is no reason to believe that solutions should be similar, although there is reason to believe that they would tend to converge over time as the cost of information fell. However, after ten thousand years of civilization, despite the immense decline in information costs and despite the implications of neoclassical international trade models that would suggest convergence, there is enormous contrast between economies.

Which brings me to the second issue. What accounts for the survival of societies and economies that are characterized by persistent poor performance? Since Charles Darwin, evolutionary theory has had a powerful influence upon our understanding of social survival, and it has been embedded in the literature of economics since the publication of Armen Alchian's 1950 article. The implications of the theory are that over time inefficient institutions are weeded out, efficient ones survive, and thus there is a gradual evolution of more efficient forms of economic, political, and social organization.

I have used the term efficient in this study to indicate a condition where the existing set of constraints will produce economic growth. Specifically, institutions that enable the parties in the exchange to capture more of the gains from trade will grow relative to those that fail to realize this potential. Either emigration to the more successful economies or emulation of the institutions of those economies would result. Again going back to the Coase theorem: in a world of zero transaction costs, the efficient solution that produced the highest aggregate income would prevail. But because transaction costs are not zero, we could anticipate differential performance reflecting different degrees of success of institutional frameworks in reducing transaction (and transformation) costs. But why would the relatively inefficient economies persist? What prevents them from adopting the institutions of the more efficient economies?

If institutions existed in the zero transaction cost framework, then history would not matter; a change in relative prices or preferences would induce an immediate restructuring of institutions to adjust efficiently, as described in Chapter 2 on the competitive model. But if the process by which we arrive at today's institutions is relevant and constrains future choices, then not only does history matter but persistent poor performance and long-run divergent patterns of development stem from a common source.

I

As a first approximation to dealing with these issues, I turn to an interesting body of economic literature that has focused primarily on the evolution of technology, but has made analogies to a broader range of questions, including, although mostly implicitly, institutional change. The article that first called the attention of economic historians to the issue of path dependence is Paul David's "Clio and the Economics of QWERTY" (1985). In this article, David attempts to explain how the peculiar organization of letters on the typewriter keyboard became standardized and fixed and to explain what accidental set of happenings appears to have caused this result to persist, even in the face of more efficient alternatives. Technological anomalies of this kind are not hard to find. The persistence of narrow-gauge rails, the success of alternating current over direct current, and the survival of the gas engine over steam engine motor cars have all been used to illustrate the peculiar fact that incremental changes in technology, once begun on a particular track, may lead one technological solution to win out over another, even when, ultimately, this technological path may be less efficient than the abandoned alternative would have been.

The argument that small historical events can lead one technology to win out over another was developed first by W. Brian Arthur.[1] I elaborate

---

[1] For a brief survey of Arthur's arguments and a summary of a substantial amount of his work, see his "Self-Reinforcing Mechanisms in Economics," in a volume called *The Economy as An Evolving Complex System* (1988).

the argument along the lines he set down. Let us examine, side by side, two competing technologies that both yield increasing returns. Agents apply learning by doing to these separate technologies, improving the efficiency of each in a manner analogous to the way organizations evolve (see Chapter 9). Each agent adapts more efficient ways of solving problems and of utilizing new technologies and equipment, and yet we may not be able to predict which technology will turn out to be the most efficient one. Because the rate of increasing returns may not remain constant for both, however, they may not grow at the same rate. Moreover, subsequent breakthroughs in one technology, unknown to the players originally, may result in monopolistic domination of the other because increasing returns imply a single winner over time. Or, simply, some small event may give one technology an advantage over the other. Hence, one technology will win out and maintain a monopolistic position, even though its successful innovations may turn out, downstream, to be inferior (or a blind alley) compared to the abandoned alternative technology. Arthur has in mind four self-reinforcing mechanisms: (1) large setup or fixed costs, which give the advantage of falling unit costs as output increases; (2) learning effects, which improve products or lower their costs as their prevalence increases; (3) coordination effects, which confer advantages to cooperation with other economic agents taking similar action; and (4) adaptive expectations, where increased prevalence on the market enhances beliefs of further prevalence.[2]

The consequence of these self-reinforcing mechanisms is, in Arthur's terms, characterized by four properties: (1) multiple equilibria – a number of solutions are possible and the outcome is indeterminate; (2) possible inefficiencies – a technology that is inherently better than another loses out because of bad luck in gaining adherence; (3) lock-in – once reached, a solution is difficult to exit from; (4) path dependence – the consequence of small events and chance circumstances can determine solutions that, once they prevail, lead one to a particular path.

Can one extend this argument of technological change to institutional change? To review its assumptions: Arthur deals with competitive markets in which agents respond to maximizing opportunities; he is analyzing competing technologies, both of which are subject to increasing returns. In fact (although I am not aware that Arthur makes this distinction), the competition is only indirectly between technologies. Directly it is between organizations embodying the competing technologies. The distinction is important because the outcome may reflect differing organizational abilities (tacit knowledge of the entrepreneurs) as much as specific aspects of the competing technologies. Indeed, ultimately Arthur is

[2]Arthur (1988), p. 10.

dealing with decision making in organizations, as is the institutional model of this study.

II

There are two forces shaping the path of institutional change: increasing returns and imperfect markets characterized by significant transaction costs. Although Arthur's technological story is coextensive with the first, neither he nor David explicitly deals with the second. I shall deal with them in turn.

In a world in which there are no increasing returns to institutions and markets are competitive, institutions do not matter. If, as discussed in Chapter 2, the actors initially have incorrect models and act upon them, they either will be eliminated or efficient information feedback will induce them to modify their models.

But, with increasing returns, institutions matter. Indeed, all four of Arthur's self-reinforcing mechanisms apply, although with somewhat different characteristics. There are large initial setup costs when the institutions are created de novo as was the U.S. Constitution in 1787. There are significant learning effects for organizations that arise in consequence of the opportunity set provided by the institutional framework (as elaborated in Chapter 9). The resultant organizations will evolve to take advantage of the opportunities defined by that framework, but as in the case of technology, there is no implication that the skills acquired will result in increased social efficiency. There will be coordination effects directly via contracts with other organizations and indirectly by induced investment through the polity in complementary activities. Even more important, the formal rules will result in the creation of a variety of informal constraints that modify the formal rules and extend them to a variety of specific applications. Adaptive expectations occur because increased prevalence of contracting based on a specific institution will reduce uncertainties about the permanence of that rule. In short, the interdependent web of an institutional matrix produces massive increasing returns.

With increasing returns, institutions matter and shape the long-run path of economies, but as long as the consequent markets are competitive or even roughly approximate the zero-transaction-cost model, the long-run path is an efficient one as that term has been used here. Given reasonably noncontroversial assumptions about preferences, neither divergent paths nor persistently poor performance would prevail. But if the markets are incomplete, the information feedback is fragmentary at best, and transaction costs are significant, then the subjective models of actors modified both by very imperfect feedback and by ideology will shape the path. Then, not only can both divergent paths and persistently poor performance prevail, the historically derived perceptions of the actors shape the choices that they make. In a dynamic world characterized by institutional increasing returns, the imperfect and fumbling efforts of the actors reflect the difficulties of deciphering a complex environment with the available mental constructs – ideas, theories, and ideologies.

We return to the institutional evolution occurring in medieval and early modern Western Europe briefly described in Chapter 10. The radical decline in population in the fourteenth century altered the bargaining strength of peasants vis-à-vis lords and led to incremental alterations over time in the implicit contracts between them. The margins at which alterations occurred can only be understood in terms of the historically derived costs of transacting and the historically derived *models* that both parties possessed about their worlds. The transaction costs were embodied in the customs of the manor, which had evolved over time in defining the relationship of lord to serf. The historically derived model that each possessed of his world included a status relationship of inequality characterized by a master-servant status; neither party would have even envisioned a change that would have eliminated that inequality. The incremental changes are only intelligible in terms of these historical relationships. If institutions were not subject to increasing returns and subjective perceptions were always corrected to true models, then presumably the actors would immediately have recontracted to a far more efficient joint solution. In fact, because there were increasing returns to the institutional framework, the process was incremental and, as described earlier, consisted of a slow evolution of formal and informal constraints and enforcement changes. And because, in this particular instance, competitive political forces and very slowly changing mental constructs of the status of both parties combined to produce more efficient outcomes (both in agriculture and in commerce), we tell it as a success story entitled *The Rise of the Western World*.

But it is still an exceptional story in economic history (see Chapter 13). Throughout most of history the experience of the agents and the ideologies of the actors do not combine to lead to efficient outcomes. Before systematically examining the sources of persistently inefficient paths, I shall attempt to make the process of path dependence clearer with several illustrations.

III

The evolution of the common law, a form of institutional change, is helpful in understanding overall institutional change. Common law is precedent based – it provides continuity and essential predictability that are critical to reducing uncertainty among contracting parties. Past decisions become embedded in the structure of law, which changes marginally as new cases arise involving new, or at least in terms of past cases unforeseen, issues; when decided these become, in turn, a part of the legal framework. The judicial decisions reflect the subjective processing of information in the context of the historical construction of the legal framework. Now if, in fact, the common law is efficient, as a number of modern law and economics scholars have asserted, it would be because the competitive process does indeed lead the judicial actors to correct models. But if the judicial decision makers operate on the basis of incomplete information and their subjective and ideologically conditioned views of how the world ought to be, then no such assertion should be made.[3] However we account for the judicial process, the institutional framework is being continuously but incrementally modified by the purposive activities of organizations bringing cases before the courts.

The Northwest Ordinance, a specific legislative enactment, illustrates the historically derived continuity implied by path dependence as well as the downstream consequences of increasing returns. The act itself was a law of fundamental importance to the development of the polity and economy of the United States. It was passed in 1787 by the Continental Congress at the very time that the Constitutional Convention was meeting in Philadelphia. The ordinance was the third act to deal with a whole range of issues concerned with the governance and settlement of the vast area of land in the West and provided a framework by which the territories would be integrated into the new nation. It will be useful to describe the ordinance, where the rules came from, how they were incorporated, and how they relate to the issues of path dependence.

The ordinance is quite simple and brief. It provided for rules of inheritance and fee-simple ownership of land and it set up the basic structure of the territorial governments and provided for the mechanisms by which territories gradually became self-governing. Additionally, it made provisions for when a territory could be admitted as a state. Then there were a series of articles of compact, in effect a bill of rights for the territories (i.e., provisions for religious freedom, the writ of habeas corpus, trial by jury, bailment, enforcement of contract, and compensation for property). There were additional provisions about good faith to the Indians, free navigation on the Mississippi and the St. Lawrence, public debt, land

---

[3]In "Imperfect Decisions and the Law: On the Evolution of Legal Precedent and Rules," Heiner (1986) makes the point forcefully in his analysis of the evolution of common law that as agents increasingly must interpret less familiar "non-local" (to use Heiner's term) information, they process it imperfectly. Hence, legal precedent establishes relatively simple standards that a judge can follow. Such a conclusion is in sharp contrast to the *efficient* consequences of common law that are characteristic of much of the law and economics research.

disposal, the number of states that could be divided up within the Northwest Territory, and finally a provision prohibiting slavery (though the return of runaway slaves was provided for) in the territories.

It is easy to trace the source of most of the provisions. The subjective models of the authors of the ordinance can be directly traced to the historical evolution of English and colonial thought (Hughes, 1987). The specific provisions had become a part of the rules of political units of the colonies during the previous 150 years. These included inheritance laws, fee-simple ownership of land, and many of the provisions of the Bill of Rights. Some, however, although precedent-based, had become controversial because legislators foresaw that the organizations (in this case states) that they represented would be affected by them – for example, provisions about the size of new states and the conditions for their admittance. The precedence was derived from the original provisions of charters and from the Articles of Confederation, but controversies arose because the conditions for admitting territories into states would critically influence the relative power and bargaining strength of existing states. One of the rules, the prohibition of slavery, appears to have been the result of vote trading between the authors of the Northwest Ordinance and the writers of the Constitution; slavery was prohibited in the former bill in return for counting slaves as three-fifths of a person in the Constitution, which increased the representation of Southern slave states in Congress (a major issue of the period).

The Northwest Ordinance provided the basic framework dictating the pattern of expansion of the United States over the next century. Although its provisions were at times modified by new issues and controversies, it provided a clear, path-dependent pattern of institutional evolution. The increasing-returns characteristics stemmed from the fact that the structure of property rights, inheritance laws, and political decision rules in the territories was derived from the act and in turn spawned organizations and (political and economic) entrepreneurs who induced marginal alterations in the act downstream. Indeed, the very success of the act was reflected in the growing influence of new Western territories and states and successful efforts by their representatives to modify land policy in their interests (North and Rutten, 1987). Therefore, U.S. land history is only understandable as a story of incremental institutional change involving interplay between the institutional framework and the consequent organizations.

If, however, the foregoing story sounds like an inevitable, foreordained account, it should not. At every step along the way there were choices – political and economic – that provided real alternatives. Path dependence is a way to narrow conceptually the choice set and link decision making through time. It is not a story of inevitability in which the past neatly predicts the future. In the story briefly recounted above, the pieces of the bill were in part derived from the colonial charters, but the final bill was significantly altered as a result of (1) conflicts among the states over entry conditions of the territories (which would determine the subsequent bargaining position of existing states), (2) the North/South issues over slavery, and (3) the coincidental Constitutional Convention in Philadelphia.

We can now integrate the path-dependent character of the incremental change in institutions with the persistence of patterns of long-run growth or decline. Once a development path is set on a particular course, the network externalities, the learning process of organizations, and the historically derived subjective modeling of the issues reinforce the course. In the case of economic growth, an adaptively efficient path, as described in Chapter 9, allows for a maximum of choices under uncertainty, for the pursuit of various trial methods of undertaking activities, and for an efficient feedback mechanism to identify choices that are relatively inefficient and to eliminate them. Note that the Northwest Ordinance not only provided adaptively efficient economic development – by fee-simple ownership of land and a clear system of inheritance that in turn made the transferability of land possible at low transaction costs – it also provided an efficient system of government, which allowed for the political transaction costs of integrating the territories into the national government to be low. Indeed, it is not too much to say that despite the inefficiencies of some specific subsequent land acts in the nineteenth century, the basic provisions of the Northwest Ordinance provided for relatively efficient solutions to these problems with the easy transfer of land, so that no matter how inappropriately we may have devised land distribution schemes later on, their costs were minimized to a substantial degree by the basic provisions of the Northwest Ordinance.

But so, too, can unproductive paths persist. The increasing returns characteristic of an initial set of institutions that provide disincentives to productive activity will create organizations and interest groups with a stake in the existing constraints. They will shape the polity in their interests. Such institutions provide incentives that may encourage military domination of the polity and economy, religious fanaticism, or plain, simple redistributive organizations, but they provide few rewards from increases in the stock and dissemination of economically useful knowledge. The subjective mental constructs of the participants will evolve an ideology that not only rationalizes the society's structure but accounts for its poor performance. As a result the economy will evolve policies that reinforce the existing incentives and organizations. Thus, both the writings of the Economic Commission for Latin America (ECLA) and dependency theory explain the poor performance of Latin American economies on the basis of the international terms of trade with industrial countries and other conditions external to those economies. Such an explanation not only rationalizes the structure of Latin American economies, but also contains policy implications that would reinforce the existing institutional framework.

Because all economies have institutional frameworks that create both productive and unproductive opportunities for organizations, the history of any economy will reflect some mixed results. Recall that the immediate instruments of institutional change are political or economic entrepreneurs who attempt to maximize at those margins that appear to offer the most profitable (short-run) alternatives. Whether the most promising alternative is investing in piracy, constructing an oil cartel, or developing a more high-powered chip for computers, it is the existing constraints and changes in incentives at the margin that determine opportunities. But note that the agent – the entrepreneur – not only is constrained in alternatives by the existing institutions, but has imperfect knowledge with respect to accomplishing his or her objective. Therefore, even if – a *big* if – the objective happened to be consistent with increasing productivity, there is no guarantee that the goal would be realized, and unexpected consequences could lead to radically different results (a technological breakthrough that made property rights more insecure or increased the payoffs to terrorism, for example). In effect, short-run efforts at profit maximizing may result in the pursuit of persistently inefficient activities (given the institutional constraints) and, even if they pursue productive activities, may have unexpected consequences. (This can, of course, work in the other direction too; pirates might eventually find that settlement and trade turned out to be more profitable, as the Vikings did.)

However, it would be a mistake to think that successful paths get reversed by small events or errors and vice versa. Recall the increasing-returns nature of the institutional matrix made up of a complex of interdependent rules and informal constraints that in total determine economic performance; individual, specific changes in formal or informal constraints certainly may change history, but for the most part do not reverse its direction. The brief account of United States land policy makes clear that although specific acts were inefficient, the overall institutional framework (comprising not only the Northwest Ordinance, but the two preceding ordinances, the complementary provisions embodied in the United States Constitution, and the equally complementary informal constraints that had evolved) reduced their inefficient consequences.

Path dependence means that history matters. We cannot understand today's choices (and define them in the modeling of economic performance) without tracing the incremental evolution of institutions. But we are just beginning the serious task of exploring the implications of path dependence.

IV

Why does a fundamental change in relative prices affect two societies differently? The answer should now be clear. In each society the change will result in adaptations at the margin, and the margins affected will be those where the immediate issues require solution and the solution will be determined by the relative bargaining power of the participants – that is, the organizations that have evolved in the specific overall institutional context. But note that it will be a marginal adjustment, built upon the preceding institutional arrangements. Because the bargaining power of groups in one society will clearly differ from that in another, the marginal adjustments in each society will typically be different as well. Moreover, with different past histories and incomplete feedback on the consequences, the actors will have different subjective models and therefore make different policy choices. Marginal adjustment in such cases does not lead to convergence.

What happens when a common set of rules is imposed on two different societies? I can illustrate from an historical example. The U.S. Constitution was adopted (with modifications) by many Latin American countries in the nineteenth century, and many of the property rights laws of successful Western countries have been adopted by Third World countries. The results, however, are not similar to those in either the United States or other successful Western countries. Although the rules are the same, the enforcement mechanisms, the way enforcement occurs, the norms of behavior, and the subjective models of the actors are not. Hence, both the real incentive structures and the perceived consequences of policies will differ as well. Thus, a common set of fundamental changes in relative prices or the common imposition of a set of rules will lead to widely divergent outcomes in societies with different institutional arrangements.

V

The focus of this chapter has been on gradual institutional change occurring through continuous marginal adjustments. The emphasis on this type of change is deliberate. It is the dominant way by which societies and economies have evolved. But as briefly discussed in the preceding chapter, discontinuous institutional change by conquest or revolution is also important. Such institutional discontinuities only reinforce my argument, however, because the tenacious survival of institutional constraints in the face of radical alterations in the formal rules of the game is the best evidence of the increasing-returns characteristics of an institutional framework. For example, take the revolutions that swept North and South America and created independence from Britain and Spain in the eighteenth and early nineteenth centuries. The evolution of North America and of Latin America differed radically right from the beginning, reflecting the imposition of the institutional patterns from the mother country upon the colonies and the radically divergent ideological constructs that shape the perceptions of the actors.

In the case of North America, the English colonies were formed in the very century when the struggle between Parliament and the Crown was coming to a head. Religious diversity as well as political diversity in the mother country were paralleled in the colonies and were reflected in the ideas and models that came to be eloquently articulated in the eighteenth century. There was substantial diversity in the political structure of crown, proprietary, and charter colonies, but the general development in the direction of local political control and the growth of assemblies was clear and unambiguous. Similarly, the navigation acts placed the colonies within the framework of overall British imperial policy. But within that broad framework, the colonists were free to develop their own economy. Indeed, sometimes the colonists themselves imposed more restrictions on property rights than did the mother country.

The French and Indian War (1756 to 1763) is a familiar breaking point in U.S. history. British efforts to impose a very modest tax on colonial subjects, as well as to curb westward migration, produced a violent reaction. The subjective perception of many colonists was that the British navigation acts threatened the prosperity of the colonies. In fact, the burden of the navigation acts was negligible and it is reasonable to presume that had the colonies remained a part of Britain, as Canada did, they would have prospered. But the perception of the colonists was different, and their acting on that perception led – via steps taken by individuals and organizations – to the Revolutionary War, the Declaration of Independence, the Articles of Confederation, the Northwest Ordinance, and the Constitution, a sequence of institutional expressions that formed a consistent evolutionary institutional pattern. Yet although the revolution created the United States, postrevolutionary history is only intelligible in terms of the continuity of informal and, indeed, many formal institutional constraints carried over from before the revolution.

In the case of the Spanish Indies, conquest came at the precise time that the influence of the Castilian Cortes was declining, the conquerors imposed a uniform religion and a uniform bureaucratic administration on an already existing agricultural society (particularly in the highlands of Mexico and Alto Peru, where agricultural societies were well developed), the bureaucracy detailed every aspect of political and economic policy (again much more stringently and effectively applied in the populated and valued regions than in the nomadic and empty areas), and there were recurrent crises over the problems of agency and control of the bureaucratic machinery. Although efforts at reversing the centralized bureaucratic policy occurred under the Bourbons and even to some extent led to the liberalization of trade within the empire, the reversal was partial and quickly negated. The control of agents was a persistent problem compounded by the efforts of the Creoles to take over the bureaucracy to pursue their own interests. Although the Wars of Independence turned out to be a struggle for control of the bureaucracy and consequent polity and economy between local colonial control and imperial control, nevertheless the struggle was imbued with the ideological overtones that stemmed from the U.S. and French revolutions. As a consequence, independence brought U.S.-inspired constitutions, but the results were radically different.

In the case of the United States, the Constitution embodied the ongoing heritage of first British and then colonial economic and political policies complemented by a consistent ideological modeling of the issues. In the case of Latin America, an alien set of rules was imposed on a long heritage of centralized bureaucratic controls and accompanying ideological perceptions of the issues. In consequence, Latin American federal schemes and efforts at decentralization did not work after the first few years of independence. The gradual reversion, country by country, to bureaucratic centralized control characterized Latin America in the nineteenth and the twentieth centuries. The persistence of the institutional pattern that had been imposed by Spain and Portugal continued to play a fundamental role in the evolution of Latin American policies and perceptions and to distinguish that continent's history, despite the imposition after independence of a set of rules similar to the British institutional tradition that shaped the path of North America.[4]

VI

Technological change and institutional change are the basic keys to societal and economic evolution and both exhibit the characteristics of path dependence. Can a single model account for both technological and institutional change? They do have much in common. Increasing returns is an essential ingredient to both. The perceptions of the actors play a more central role in institutional than in technological change because ideological beliefs influence the subjective construction of the models that determine choices. Choices are more multifaceted in an institutional context because of the complex interrelationships among formal and informal

[4]For a summary account of the Latin American experience see C. Veliz, *The Centralist Tradition in Latin America* (1980) or W. G. Glade, *The Latin American Economies: A Study of Their Institutional Evolution* (1969).

constraints. In consequence, both lock-in and path dependence appear much more complicated in the case of institutions than in the case of technology. The interplay between the polity and the economy, the many actors who have varying degrees of bargaining strength in influencing institutional change, and the role of cultural inheritance that appears to underlie the persistence of many informal constraints all contribute to this complexity.

I conclude this chapter by emphasizing some implications of this analysis. Long-run economic change is the cumulative consequence of innumerable short-run decisions by political and economic entrepreneurs that both directly and indirectly (via external effects) shape performance. The choices made reflect the entrepreneurs' subjective modeling of the environment. Therefore, the degree to which outcomes are consistent with intentions will reflect the degree to which the entrepreneur's models are *true* models. Because the models reflect ideas, ideologies, and beliefs that are, at best, only partially refined and improved by information feedback on the actual consequences of the enacted policies, the consequences of specific policies are not only uncertain but to a substantial degree unpredictable. Even the most casual inspection of political and economic choices, both throughout history and today, makes clear the wide gap between intentions and outcomes. However, the increasing-returns characteristics of the institutional matrix and the complementary subjective models of the players suggest that although the specific short-run paths are unforeseeable, the overall direction in the long run is both more predictable and more difficult to reverse.

Part III

Economic performance

12

Institutions, economic theory, and economic performance

We cannot see, feel, touch, or even measure institutions; they are constructs of the human mind. But even the most convinced neoclassical economists admit their existence and typically make them parameters (implicitly or explicitly) in their models. Do institutions matter? Do tariffs, regulations, and rules matter? Does government make a difference? Can we explain the radical change in economic well-being when we step across the boundary between the United States and Mexico? What makes markets work or not work? Does honesty in exchange make a difference; does it pay? I hope that the analysis of the previous chapters has provided a convincing framework to shed light on the consequences of institutions.

But I wish to assert a much more fundamental role for institutions in societies; they are the underlying determinant of the long-run performance of economies. If we are ever to construct a dynamic theory of change — something missing in mainstream economics and only very imperfectly dealt with in Marxian theory — it must be built on a model of institutional change. Although some of the pieces of the puzzle are still missing, the outline of the direction to be taken is, I believe, clear.

In the sections that follow I (1) specify what changes must be made in neoclassical theory to incorporate institutional analysis into that theory, (2) outline the implications for the *static* analysis of economic performance, and (3) explore the implications of institutional analysis for the construction of a dynamic theory of long-run economic change.

I

Information processing by the actors as a result of the costliness of transacting underlies the formation of institutions. At issue are both the meaning of rationality and the characteristics of transacting that prevent the actors from achieving the joint maximization result of the zero transaction cost model.

Economic performance

The instrumental rationality postulate of neoclassical theory assumes that the actors possess information necessary to evaluate correctly the alternatives and in consequence make choices that will achieve the desired ends. In fact, such a postulate has implicitly assumed the existence of a particular set of institutions and information. If institutions play a purely passive role so that they do not constrain the choices of the actors and the actors are in possession of the information necessary to make correct choices, then the instrumental rationality postulate is the correct building block. If, on the other hand, the actors are incompletely informed, devise subjective models as guides to choices, and can only very imperfectly correct their models with information feedback, then a procedural rationality postulate (as described in Chapter 3) is the essential building block to theorizing.

The former postulate evolved in the context of the highly developed, efficient markets of the Western world and has served as a useful tool of analysis in such a context. But those markets are characterized by the exceptional condition of low or negligible transaction costs. I know of no way to analyze most markets in the contemporary world and throughout history with such a behavioral postulate. A procedural rationality postulate, on the other hand, not only can account for the incomplete and imperfect markets that characterize much of the present and the past world, but also leads the researcher to the key issues of just what it is that makes markets imperfect. That leads us to the costs of transacting.

The costs of transacting arise because information is costly and asymmetrically held by the parties to exchange and also because any way that the actors develop institutions to structure human interaction results in some degree of imperfection of the markets. In effect, the incentive consequences of institutions provide mixed signals to the participants, so that even in those cases where the institutional framework is conducive to capturing more of the gains from trade as compared to an earlier institutional framework, there will still be incentives to cheat, free ride, and so forth that will contribute to market imperfections. Given the behavioral characteristics of human beings, there is simply no way to devise institutions that solve the complex exchange problems and at the same time are free of some incompatible incentives. As a result, much of the recent literature of industrial organization and political economy has attempted to come to grips with incentive incompatibility in economic and political organization (see Miller, *Managerial Dilemmas: The Political Economy of Hierarchies,* forthcoming). The success stories of economic history describe the institutional innovations that have lowered the costs of transacting and permitted capturing more of the gains from trade and hence permitted the expansion of markets. But such innovations, for the most part, have not created the conditions necessary for the efficient markets of the neoclassical model. The polity specifies and enforces the property rights of the economic marketplace, and the characteristics of the political market are the essential key to understanding the imperfections of markets.

What would make the political market approximate the zero transaction cost model for efficient economic exchange? The condition is easily stated. Legislation would be enacted which increased aggregate income and in which the gainers compensated losers at a transaction cost that is low enough to make it jointly worthwhile. The informational and institutional conditions necessary to realize such exchange are:

1. The affected parties must have the information and correct model to know that the bill affects them and to know the amount of gains or losses they would incur.
2. The results can be communicated to their agent (the legislator) who will faithfully vote accordingly.
3. Votes will be weighted by the aggregate net gains or losses so that the net result can be ascertained and the losers appropriately compensated.
4. This exchange can be accomplished at a low enough cost of transacting to make it worthwhile.

The institutional structure most favorable to approximating such conditions is a modern democratic society with universal suffrage. Vote trading, log rolling, and the incentive of an incumbent's opponents to bring his or her *deficiencies* before constituents and hence reduce agency problems all contribute to *better* outcomes.

But look at the disincentives built into the system. Rational voter ignorance is not just a buzzword of the public choice literature. Not only could the voter never acquire the information to be even vaguely informed about the myriad bills that affect his or her welfare, but there is no way that the constituent (or even the legislator) could ever possess accurate models to weigh the consequences. Agency theory has provided abundant, if controversial, evidence of the degree to which the legislator acts independently of constituent interests. Whereas the legislator is going to trade votes on the basis of perceived number of votes he or she stands to gain or lose, that is frequently a long way from reflecting net gains or losses to all the constituents. And how often is there an incentive to compensate losers? There is a vast gap between *better* and *efficient* (in the neoclassical meaning of that term) outcomes, as a vast literature in modern political economy will attest. For my purpose, it is necessary to emphasize two essential conditions that loom large. They are that the affected parties have both the information and the correct model to accurately appraise the consequences and that all the affected parties have equal access to the decision-making process. These conditions are not even approximately met in the most favorable institutional framework in all of history for efficient political decision making.

Because polities make and enforce economic rules, it is not surprising that property rights are seldom efficient (North, 1981). But even when efficient property rights are devised, they will still typically have features that will be very costly to monitor or enforce, reflecting built-in disincentives or at the very least aspects of the exchange that provide temptation to renege, shirk, steal, or cheat. In many cases informal constraints will evolve to mitigate these disincentive consequences. And the modern Western world provides abundant evidence of markets that work and even approximate the neoclassical ideal. But they are exceptional and difficult to come by, and the institutional requirements are stringent.

II

The consequences of institutions for contemporary economic analysis can be summarized as follows:

1. Economic (and political) models are specific to particular constellations of institutional constraints that vary radically both through time and cross sectionally in different economies. The models are institution specific and in many cases highly sensitive to altered institutional constraints. A self-conscious awareness of these constraints is essential both for improved theory construction and for issues of public policy. It is not just how well would the model play in Bangladesh or in the United States during the nineteenth century, but much more immediately, how would it play in another developed country like Japan or even in the United States next year?

Even more important is that the specific institutional constraints dictate the margins at which organizations operate and hence make intelligible the interplay between the rules of the game and the behavior of the actors. If organizations – firms, trade unions, farm groups, political parties, and congressional committees to name a few – devote their efforts to *unproductive activity*, the institutional constraints have provided the incentive structure for such activity. Third World countries are poor because the institutional constraints define a set of payoffs to political/economic activity that do not encourage productive activity. Socialist economies are just beginning to appreciate that the underlying institutional framework is the source of their current poor performance and are attempting to grapple with ways to restructure the institutional framework to redirect incentives that in turn will direct organizations along productivity-increasing paths. And as for the first world, we not only need to appreciate the importance of an overall institutional framework that has been responsible for the growth of the economy, but to be self-conscious about the consequences of the ongoing marginal changes that are continually occurring– not only on overall performance but also on specific sectors of the economy. We have long been aware that the tax structure, regulations, judicial decisions, and statute laws, to name but a few formal constraints, shape the policies of firms, trade unions, and other organizations and hence determine specific aspects of economic performance; but such awareness has not led to a focusing of economic theory on modeling the political/economic process that produces these results.

2. A self-conscious incorporation of institutions will force social scientists in general, and economists in particular, to question the behavioral models that underlie their disciplines and, in consequence, to explore much more systematically than we have done so far the implications of the costly and imperfect processing of information for the consequent behavior of the actors. Social scientists have incorporated the costliness of information in their models, but have not come to grips with the subjective mental constructs by which individuals process information and arrive at conclusions that shape their choices. There is in economics a (largely) implicit assumption that the actors can correctly identify the reason for their predicaments (i.e., have *true* theories), know the costs and benefits of alternative choices, and know how to act upon them (see, for example, Becker, 1983). Our preoccupation with rational choice and efficient market hypotheses has blinded us to the implications of incomplete information and the complexity of environments and subjective perceptions of the external world that individuals hold. There is nothing the matter with the rational actor paradigm that could not be cured by a healthy awareness of the complexity of human motivation and the problems that arise from information processing. Social scientists would then understand not only why institutions exist, but also how they influence outcomes.

3. Ideas and ideologies matter, and institutions play a major role in determining just how much they matter. Ideas and ideologies shape the subjective mental constructs that individuals use to interpret the world around them and make choices. Moreover, by structuring the interaction of human beings in certain ways, formal institutions affect the price we pay for our actions, and to the degree the formal institutions are deliberately or accidentally structured to lower the price of acting on one's ideas, they provide the freedom to individuals to incorporate their ideas and ideologies into the choices they make. A key consequence of formal institutions is mechanisms, like voting systems in democracies or organizational structures in hierarchies, that enable individuals who are agents to express their own views and to have a very different impact upon outcomes than those implied by the simple interest-group modeling that has characterized so much of economic and public choice theory.

4. The polity and the economy are inextricably interlinked in any understanding of the performance of an economy and therefore we must develop a true political economy discipline. A set of institutional constraints defines the exchange relationships between the two and therefore determines the way a political/economic system works. Not only do polities specify and enforce property rights that shape the basic incentive structure of an economy, in the modern world the share of gross national product going through government and the ubiquitous and ever-changing regulations imposed by it are the most important keys to economic performance. A useful model of the macroaspect or even microaspects of an economy must build the institutional constraints into the model. Modern macroeconomic theory, for example, will never resolve the problems that it confronts unless its practitioners recognize that the decisions made by the political process critically affect the functioning of economies. Although at an ad hoc level we have begun to recognize this, much more integration of politics and economics than has been accomplished so far is needed. This can only be done by a modeling of the political-economic process that incorporates the specific institutions involved and the consequent structure of political and economic exchange.

III

Integrating institutional analysis into *static* neoclassical theory entails modifying the existing body of theory. But devising a model of economic change requires the construction of an entire theoretical framework, because no such model exists. Path dependence is the key to an analytical understanding of long-run economic change. The promise of this approach is that it extends the most constructive building blocks of neoclassical theory – both the scarcity/competition postulate and incentives as the driving force – but modifies that theory by incorporating incomplete information and subjective models of *reality* and the increasing returns characteristic of institutions. The result is an approach that offers the promise of connecting microlevel economic activity with the macrolevel incentives provided by the institutional framework. The source of incremental change is the gains to be obtained by organizations and their entrepreneurs from acquiring skills, knowledge, and information that will enhance their objectives. Path dependence comes from the increasing returns mechanisms that reinforce the direction once on a given path. Alterations in the path come from unanticipated consequences of choices, external effects, and sometimes forces exogenous to the analytical framework. Reversal of paths (from stagnation to growth or vice versa) may come from the above described sources of path alteration, but will typically occur through changes in the polity.

Economic theory and economic performance

I can expand on the sequential characteristics of path dependence by returning to the contrast between the British-North American path and the Spanish-Latin American path, discussed in Chapter 11.

The background

At the beginning of the sixteenth century, England and Spain had evolved very differently. England had developed a relatively centralized feudalism, as a result of the Norman conquest, and had recently established the Tudors with the Battle of Bosworth (1485). Spain, in contrast, had just emerged from seven centuries of Moorish domination of the Iberian Peninsula. It was not a unified country. Although the marriage of Ferdinand and Isabella brought Castile and Aragon together, they continued to maintain separate rules, Cortes, and policies.

However, both England and Spain faced, in common with the rest of the emerging European nation-states, a critical problem: the need to acquire additional revenue to survive in the face of the rising costs of warfare. The king traditionally lived on his own, that is, off the revenue from his estates together with the traditional feudal dues; but these resources were insufficient in the face of the new military technology associated with the effective use of the crossbow, longbow, pike, and gunpowder. This fiscal crisis of the state, first described by Joseph Schumpeter (1954), forced rulers to make bargains with constituents. In both countries, the consequence was the development of some form of representation on the part of constituents (Parliament in England and the Cortes in Spain) in return for revenue. In both countries, the wool trade became a major source of crown revenue. But the consequences of the common relative price change arising from the new military technology were radically different in the two countries. In one, it led to the evolution of a polity and economy that solved the fiscal crisis and went on to dominate the Western world. In the other, in spite of initially more favorable conditions, it led to unresolved fiscal crises, bankruptcies, confiscation of assets, and insecure property rights and to three centuries of relative stagnation.

In England, the tension between ruler and constituent (although the barons at Runnymede might have caviled at that term) surfaced with the Magna Carta in 1215. The fiscal crisis came later with the Hundred Years War. Stubbs describes the consequence as follows: "The admission of the right of parliament to legislate, to enquire into abuses, and to share in the guidance of national policy, was practically purchased by the money granted to Edward I and Edward III." (Stubbs, 1896, p. 599) The subsequent history to 1689 and the final triumph of Parliament is well known.

In Spain, the union of Aragon (comprising approximately Valencia, Aragon, and Catalonia) and Castile joined two very different regions. Aragon had been reconquered from the Arabs in the last half of the thirteenth century and had become a major commercial empire extending into Sardinia, Sicily, and parts of Greece. The Cortes reflected the interests of merchants and played a significant role in public affairs. In contrast, Castile was continually engaged in warfare, either against the Moors or in internal strife, and although the Cortes existed it was seldom summoned. In the fifteen years after their union, Isabella succeeded in gaining control not only over the unruly warlike barons, but over church policy in Castile as well. Although the role of the Castilian Cortes has, in recent scholarly work, been somewhat upgraded, nevertheless there was a centralized monarchy and bureaucracy in Castile, and it was Castile that defined the institutional evolution of both Spain and Latin America.

The institutional framework

It was not simply centralization or decentralization in the polity that differentiated the two societies. Nevertheless, this feature made a critical difference and was symptomatic of the broad differences in both the polity and the economy. Not only did the Parliament in England provide the beginning of representative government and a reduction in the *rent-seeking* behavior that had characterized the financially hard-pressed Stuart monarchs, but also Parliament's triumph betokened increased security of property rights and a more effective, impartial judicial system.

Spain's polity consisted of a large centralized bureaucracy that "administered the ever-growing body of decrees and juridical directives, which both legitimized the administrative machinery and laid down its course of action" (Glade, 1969, p. 58). Every detail of the economy as well as the polity was structured with the objective of furthering the interests of the crown in the creation of the most powerful empire since Rome. But with the revolt of the Netherlands and the decline in the inflow of New World treasure, the fiscal demands far outstripped revenue, and the result was bankruptcy, increased internal taxation, confiscations, and insecure property rights.

The organizational implications

In England, Parliament created the Bank of England and a fiscal system in which expenditures were tied to tax revenues. The consequent financial revolution not only finally put the government on a sound financial basis, but laid the ground for the development of the private capital market. More secure property rights, the decline of mercantilist restrictions, and the escape of textile firms from urban guild restrictions combined to provide expanding opportunities for firms in domestic and international markets. Both the growing markets and the patent law encouraged the growth of innovative activity. But all this and much more is a familiar story.

Economic theory and economic performance

In Spain, repeated bankruptcies between 1557 and 1647 were coupled with desperate measures to stave off disaster. War, the church, and administering the complex bureaucratic system provided the major organizational opportunities in Spain and in consequence the military, priesthood, and the judiciary were rewarding occupations. The expulsion of the Moors and Jews, rent ceilings on land and price ceilings on wheat, confiscations of silver remittances to merchants in Seville (who were compensated with relatively worthless bonds called *juros*) were symptomatic of the disincentives to productive activity.

Path dependence

To make the contrasting brief stories convincing illustrations of path dependence would entail an account of the political, economic, and judicial systems of each society as a web of interconnected formal rules and informal constraints that together made up the institutional matrix and led the economies down different paths. It would be necessary to demonstrate the network externalities that limited the actors' choices and prevented them from radically altering the institutional framework. Such an undertaking is far beyond the kinds of existing empirical evidence with which I am familiar. I can only indirectly infer such implications from the evidence.

In a controversial study, *The Origins of English Individualism* (1978), Alan Macfarlane maintains that at least from the thirteenth century the English were different than the traditional picture we possess of peasant societies. The traditional characteristics – patriarchal domination, extended family, low status of women, tight knit and closed peasant villages, self-sufficiency, and the family as the work unit – all were conspicuously absent by the thirteenth century. Instead, Macfarlane paints a picture of a fluid, individualistically oriented set of attitudes involving the structure of the family, the organization of work, and the social relationships of the village community complemented by an array of formal rules dealing with property, inheritance, and the legal status of women. Macfarlane wants to make the point that England was different and that the difference went way back in time, but in doing so he amasses evidence to make clear the complex interdependent network of formal and informal constraints that made for the increasing returns characteristic of path dependence.

The most telling evidence of the increasing returns feature of the Spanish institutional fabric was the inability of the crown and its bureaucracy to alter the direction of the Spanish path in spite of their awareness of the decay and decline overcoming the country. In a century – the seventeenth – Spain declined from the most powerful nation in the Western world since the Roman empire to a second-rate power. The depopulation of the countryside, the stagnation of industry, and the collapse of Seville's trading system with the New World were paralleled in the political realm by the revolt of Catalonia and Portugal. The proximate cause was recurrent war and a fiscal crisis that led Olivares (1621 to 1640) to pursue the desperate measures that only exacerbated the fundamental problems. Indeed, the policies that were considered feasible in the context of the institutional constraints and perceptions of the actors were price controls, tax increases, and repeated confiscations. As for the perceptions of the actors, Jan De Vries in his study (1976) of Europe in the age of crisis describes the effort to reverse the decline as follows:

> But this was not a society unaware of what was happening. A whole school of economic reformers . . . wrote mountains of tracts pleading for new measures. . . . Indeed, in 1623 a *Junta de Reformacion* recommended to the new King, Philip IV, a series of measures including taxes to encourage earlier marriage (and, hence, population growth), limitations on the number of servants, the establishment of a bank, prohibitions on the import of luxuries, the closing of brothels, and the prohibition of the teaching of Latin in small towns (to reduce the flight from agriculture of peasants who had acquired a smattering of education). But no willpower could be found to follow through on these recommendations. . . . It is said that the only accomplishment of the reform movement was the abolition of the ruff collar, a fashion which had imposed ruinous laundry bills on the aristocracy. (De Vries, 1976, p. 28)

It appears doubtful that instrumental rationality could be applied to the reasoning of the Junta.

Both England and Spain faced fiscal crises in the seventeenth century, but the contrasting paths that they took appear to have reflected deep underlying institutional characteristics of the societies.

The downstream consequences

U.S. economic history has been characterized by a federal political system, checks and balances, and a basic structure of property rights that have encouraged the long-term contracting essential to the creation of capital markets and economic growth. Even one of the most costly civil wars in all of history failed to alter the basic institutional matrix.

Latin American economic history, in contrast, has perpetuated the centralized, bureaucratic traditions carried over from its Spanish/Portuguese heritage. Here is John Coatsworth's characterization of the institutional environment of nineteenth-century Mexico:

> The interventionist and pervasively arbitrary nature of the institutional environment forced every enterprise, urban or rural, to operate in a highly politicized manner, using kinship networks, political influence, and family prestige to gain privileged access to subsidized credit, to aid various strategems for recruiting labor, to collect debts or enforce contracts, to evade taxes or circumvent the

courts, and to defend or assert titles to lands. Success or failure in the economic arena always depended on the relationship of the producer with political authorities – local officials for arranging matters close at hand and the central government of the colony for sympathetic interpretations of the law and intervention at the local level when conditions required it. Small enterprise, excluded from the system of corporate privilege and political favors, was forced to operate in a permanent state of semiclandestiny, always at the margin of the law, at the mercy of petty officials, never secure from arbitrary acts and never protected against the rights of those more powerful. (Coatsworth, 1978, p. 94)

The divergent paths established by England and Spain in the New World have not converged despite the mediating factors of common ideological influences. In the former, an institutional framework has evolved that permits the complex impersonal exchange necessary to political stability and to capture the potential economic gains of modern technology. In the latter, personalistic relationships are still the key to much of the political and economic exchange. They are a consequence of an evolving institutional framework that produces neither political stability nor consistent realization of the potential of modern technology.

13

Stability and change in economic history

Institutions provide the basic structure by which human beings through-out history have created order and attempted to reduce uncertainty in exchange. Together with the technology employed, they determine trans-action and transformation costs and hence the profitability and feasibility of engaging in economic activity. They connect the past with the present and the future so that history is a largely incremental story of institutional evolution in which the historical performance of economies can only be understood as a part of a sequential story. And they are the key to under-standing the interrelationship between the polity and the economy and the consequences of that interrelationship for economic growth (or stag-nation and decline). But just why are some forms of exchange stable while others lead to more complex and productive forms of exchange? I have discussed the theoretical issues of institutional change. Here I wish to explore the specific characteristics of historical change.

In examining stability and change in history, the initial issue is the same one posed at the beginning of this study (see Chapter 2). What combina-tion of institutions permits capturing the gains from trade inherent in the standard neoclassical (zero transaction cost) model at any moment of time? The issue is complicated enough in an ahistorical context. It is vastly more complicated in history, because rather than starting with a tabula rasa, history is always derived from past history. The path-depen-dent pattern of history, elaborated in earlier chapters, in some cases re-sulted in stable exchange patterns that did not evolve while in other cases dynamic change occurred. The argument advanced in this study is that the current forms of political, economic, and military organization and their maximizing directions are derived from the opportunity set provided by the institutional structure that in turn evolved incrementally. But some-times little or no evolution occurred. Why stability in some instances and change in others? I will describe successively more complicated forms of economic exchange and then turn to the institutional and organizational structures necessary to realize these forms of exchange.[1]

I

I begin with local exchange within the village or even the simple exchange of hunting and gathering societies (in which men hunted and women gathered). Specialization in this world is rudimentary and self-sufficiency characterizes most individual households. A small step is trade expansion beyond the single village, in which some increase in specialization occurs (usually as a supplement to a largely self-sufficient household). As the market extends to regional trade, it not only implies the growth of multilateral trade over a large area and the creation of specialized marketplaces in which trade takes place, but it also sharply increases the number of trading partners. Although in this society the overwhelming proportion of the labor force is typically agricultural, an increasing percentage is engaged in trade and commerce.

The evolution and development of long-distance trade is characterized by a distinct change in the economic structure. Such trade entails some substantial specialization in the exchange process of individuals whose livelihood is confined to trading. It implies the early development of trading centers. These trading centers may be either temporary gathering places (as were the early fairs in Europe) or more permanent towns and cities. Some economies of scale as in, for example, plantation agriculture are characteristic in this world. Geographical specialization, in other words, begins to emerge as a major issue and some occupational specialization occurs as well.

The next stage in the expansion of the market entails more specialized producers. Economies of scale result in the beginnings of hierarchical producing organizations, with full-time workers working either in a central place or in a sequential production process. Towns and some central cities emerge, and occupational distribution of the population now shows, in addition, a substantial increase in the proportion of the labor force engaged in manufacturing and services, although the population still is predominantly agricultural. It also reflects a significant shift toward urbanization of the society.

---

[1]In an article written many years ago (North, 1955), I pointed out that many regional economies evolved from the very beginning as export economies. This is in comparison and in contrast to the old stage theories of history that we inherited from the German historical school, in which the evolution was always from local autarchy to increased specialization and division of labor. It is this last pattern described here, even though it may not be a correct characterization in many instances.

In the last stage, the one we observe in modern Western societies, specialization has increased, agriculture is a small percentage of the labor force, and gigantic markets that are national and international characterize economies. Economies of scale imply large-scale organization, not only in manufacturing but also in agriculture. Everyone lives by undertaking a specialized function and relying on the vast network of interconnected parts to provide the necessary multitude of goods and services. The occupational distribution of the labor force shifts gradually from dominance by manufacturing to dominance, eventually, by what are characterized as services. It is an overwhelmingly urban society.

II

In one way or another, we are familiar with these staged stories of economic history, whether from the German historical school or more recently from Rostow's stages of economic growth. My objective here, however, is to provide a different story about the characteristics of these stages; I examine what kinds of institutions are necessary to enable the cost of transacting and transforming to be at a level that will permit this increasing specialization and division of labor to occur.

The small-scale village trade exists within a dense social network of informal constraints that facilitates local exchange, and the costs of transacting in this context are low. Although the basic societal costs of tribal and village organization may be high, they will not be reflected in additional costs in the process of transacting. People have an intimate understanding of each other, and the threat of violence is a continuous force for preserving order because of its implications for other members of society.

As the size of the market grows, regional trade results in sharply higher transaction costs, because the dense social network is replaced by more infrequent clientization of the players; hence, more resources must be devoted to measurement and enforcement. In this world there are not, typically, central political authorities, and in the absence of any unified political structure or formal rules, religious precepts usually have imposed standards of conduct on the players. Their effectiveness in lowering the costs of transacting varies widely, depending on the degree to which these precepts are held to be binding on the players.

The growth of long-distance trade posed two distinct transaction cost problems. One is a classic problem of agency, which historically was met in the commenda and other early forms of organization by the use of kin in long-distance trade. That is, a sedentary merchant would send a relative with the cargo to negotiate sale and to obtain a return cargo. The costliness of measuring performance, the strength of kinship ties, and the price of defection all determined the outcome of such agreements. As the size and volume of trade grew, the problem became an increasingly major dilemma. The second problem was one of contract fulfillment and enforcement in alien parts of the world, where there was not any easily available way to enforce contracts. Enforcement meant not only protection of the goods and services en route from pirates or brigands, but also the enforcement of the agreement in alien territories. The development of standardized weights and measures, units of account, a medium of exchange, notaries, consuls, merchant law courts, and enclaves of foreign merchants protected by foreign princes in return for revenue were all part and parcel of the organizations, institutions, and instruments that made possible transacting and engaging in long-distance trade. A mixture of voluntary and semicoercive bodies, or at least bodies that effectively could cause ostracism of merchants who did not live up to agreements, enabled long-distance trade to occur.

The next stage, the creation of capital markets and the development of manufacturing firms with large amounts of fixed capital, entails some form of coercive political order, because as more complex and impersonal forms of interchange evolve, personal ties, voluntaristic constraints, and ostracism are no longer effective. It is not that they lose importance. They are still meaningful in our interdependent world. But the gains from defection are great enough to forestall such complex exchange in the absence of effective impersonal contracting. Secure property rights will require political and judicial organizations that effectively and impartially enforce contracts across space and time.

In the final stage, specialization entails that increasing percentages of the resources of the society be engaged in transacting, so that the transaction sector accounts for a large percentage of gross national product. This occurs because specialization in trade, finance, banking, and insurance, as well as the simple coordination of economic activity, involves an increasing proportion of the labor force. Of necessity, therefore, there are highly specialized forms of transaction organizations. International specialization and division of labor requires institutions and organizations to safeguard property rights across international boundaries so that capital markets as well as other kinds of exchange can take place with credible commitment on the part of the players.

The very schematic stages described above appear to merge one into another in a smooth story of the evolution of cooperation. But do they? Is there any necessary connection that moves the players from less complicated to more complicated forms of exchange? What is at stake in this evolution is not only that lower information costs and economies of scale together with the development of improved enforcement of contracts will permit and indeed encourage evolution from simpler to more complicated forms of exchange, but also that the organizations have the incentive to acquire knowledge and information that will induce them to evolve in more socially productive directions. But we should note very carefully that in fact through history there is no necessary reason for this development to occur. Indeed, it is possible to demonstrate that most of the early forms of exchange and organization that I have described still exist today in parts of the world. Primitive tribal societies still exist, the suq (bazaar economies engaged in regional trade) still flourishes in some parts of the world, and although the caravan trade has disappeared, its demise (as well as the gradual undermining of the other two forms of primitive exchange that is taking place) has reflected external forces rather than internal evolution.

In contrast, the development of European long-distance trade initiated a sequential internal development of more complex forms of organization. That is, the beginnings of long-distance trade induced, through lower information costs, some economies of scale and the development of local enforcement of contracts, a pattern of evolution in part of Western Europe that was in sharp contrast to the stability of the above-mentioned forms of primitive exchange. The kinds of learning and skills required to be successful in the Venetian Mediterranean trade or at the Champagne fairs or at Lubeck in the Hanseatic trade induced the creation of more sophisticated institutional arrangements. Whether we look at the evolution of the bill of exchange or follow the successive steps by which the law merchant doctrines become embedded in formal law, we find it was organizations pursuing profitable opportunities in the context of expanding trading opportunities that drove the institutional evolution.

Some economies evolved to produce a political structure that permitted the development of third-party enforcement and the complicated structure of institutions that characterizes the modern Western world. But even in Western Europe not all economies evolved in the same way. Rather, some, as in the case of Spain, came to a dead end as a consequence of political/economic policies that produced bankruptcy and disincentives to productive institutional innovation. By examining in more depth primitive forms of exchange and then, Western European development, I intend to focus on the contrasting forces that produced institutional and organizational stability in the first instance and dynamic economic change in the second.

III

In its earliest forms, human exchange could and did occur without even language; sign language and arm's length observation of the goods (at least as Herodotus tells it) each served as a basis of exchange. Regular exchange existed without a state, and rules of exchange were enforced by the threat of feuds between family groups. However, exchange in tribal society is not simple. The absence of a state supported by formal written rules is made up for by a dense social network. Because I described this form of exchange in Chapter 5, I shall only add here another brief quote from Elizabeth Colson (1974):

The communities in which all these people live were governed by a delicate balance of power, always endangered and never to be taken for granted: each person was constantly involved in securing his own position in situations where he had to show his good intentions. Usages and customs appear to be flexible and fluid given that judgement on whether or not someone has done rightly varies from case to case . . . . But this is because it is the individual who is being judged and not the crime. Under these conditions a flouting of generally accepted standards is tantamount to a claim to illegitimate power and becomes part of the evidence against one. (Colson, 1974, p. 59)

The implication of Colson's analysis as well as that of Richard Posner (1980) is that deviance and innovation are viewed as a threat to group survival.

A second form of exchange – the suq – has existed for thousands of years and still exists today in North Africa and the Middle East and is characterized by widespread, relatively impersonal exchange and relatively high costs of transacting.[2] The basic characteristics are a multiplicity of small-scale enterprises with as much as 40 to 50 percent of the town's labor force engaged in this exchange process, low fixed costs, a very finely drawn division of labor, an enormous number of small transactions (each more or less independent of the next), face to face contacts, and goods and services that are not homogeneous. There are no institutions specifically devoted to assembling and distributing market information. Systems of weights and measures are intricate and incompletely standardized. Exchange skills are very elaborately developed; differential possession of them is marked and is the primary determinant of who prospers in the bazaar and who does not. Haggling over terms with respect to any aspect or condition of exchange is pervasive, strenuous, and unremitting. Buying and selling are virtually undifferentiated, essentially a single activity; trading involves a continual search for specific partners, not the mere offer of goods to the general public. Regulation of disputes involves the testimony by reliable witnesses to factual matters, not the weighting of competing, juridical principles. Governmental controls over marketplace activity are marginal, decentralized, and mostly rhetorical.

[2]There is an extensive literature on the suq. I have particularly relied on a sophisticated analysis focused on the suq at Sefrou, Morocco, contained in Geertz, Geertz, and Rosen (1979).

To summarize, the central features of the suq are (1) high measurement costs, (2) continuous effort at clientization — that is, the development of repeat-exchange relationships with other partners that, however, are imperfect at best, and (3) intensive bargaining at every margin — the key is men seeking gains at the expense of others. In essence, the name of the game is to raise the costs of transacting to the other party to exchange. One makes money by having better information than one's adversary.

It is easy to understand why innovation would be seen as a threat to survival in a tribal society, but harder to understand why these inefficient forms of bargaining would continue in the suq. One would anticipate that in the societies with which we are familiar, voluntary organizations would evolve to ensure against the hazards and uncertainties of such information asymmetries. But that is precisely the issue. Missing in the suq are the fundamental underpinnings of legal institutions and judicial enforcement that would make such voluntary organizations viable and profitable. In their absence, there is no incentive to alter the system.

How did trade exist in a world where protection was essential and no organized state existed? The caravan trades illustrate the elaborate informal constraints that made such trade possible. Clifford Geertz (1979) provides us with a description of caravan trades in Morocco at the turn of the century.

In the narrow sense, a zettata (from the Berber TAZETTAT, 'a small piece of cloth') is a passage tool, a sum paid to a local power . . . for protection when crossing localities where he is such a power. But in fact it is, or more properly was, rather more than a mere payment. It was part of a whole complex of moral rituals, customs with the force of law and the weight of sanctity — centering around the guest-host, client-patron, petitioner-petitioned, exile-protector, suppliant-divinity relations — all of which are somehow of a package in rural Morocco. Entering the tribal world physically, the outreaching trader (or at least his agents) had also to enter it culturally.

Despite the vast variety of particular forms through which they manifest themselves, the characteristics of protection in the Berber societies of the High and Middle Atlas are clear and constant. Protection is personal, unqualified, explicit, and conceived of as the dressing of one man in the reputation of another. The reputation may be political, moral, spiritual, or even idiosyncratic, or, often enough, all four at once. But the essential transaction is that a man who counts 'stands up and says' (quam wa qal, as the classical tag has it) to those to whom he counts: 'This man is mine; harm him and you insult me; insult me and you will answer for it.' Benediction (the famous baraka), hospitality, sanctuary, and safe passage are alike in this: They rest on the perhaps somewhat paradoxical notion that though personal identity is radically individual in both its roots and its expressions, it is not incapable of being stamped onto the self of someone else. (Geertz, 1979, p. 137)

IV

Tribal organization, the suq, and caravan trade are characteristic of stable patterns of very limited cooperation that have persisted through history. In each case, the skills and knowledge requisite to success on the part of the organizations or individuals involved did not entail or induce productive modifications of the basic institutional framework. In each case the sources of institutional change were external.

In contrast, the history of long-distance trade in early modern Europe was the story of sequentially more complex organization that eventually led to the rise of the Western world. I will first briefly describe the innovations and then explore some of the underlying sources.

Innovations that lowered transaction costs consisted of organizational innovations, instruments, and specific techniques and enforcement characteristics. These innovations occurred at three cost margins: (1) those that increased the mobility of capital, (2) those that lowered information costs, and (3) those that spread risk. Obviously these are overlapping categories; however, they provide a useful way to distinguish cost-reducing features of transacting. All of these innovations had their origins in earlier times; most of them were borrowed from medieval Italian city states or Islam or Byzantium and elaborated upon in subsequent development.

Among innovations that affected the mobility of capital were the techniques and methods evolved to evade usury law. The variety of ingenious ways by which interest was disguised in loan contracts ranged from "penalties for late payment," to exchange rate manipulation (Lopez and Raymond, 1955, p. 163), to the early form of the mortgage, but all increased the cost of contracting. The costliness of usury laws was not only that they made the writing of contracts to disguise interest complex and cumbersome, but also that enforceability of such contracts had become more problematic. As usury laws gradually broke down and higher rates of interest were permitted, the costs of writing contracts and the costs of enforcing them declined.

Also affecting the mobility of capital, and the innovation that has received the most attention, was the evolution of the bill of exchange and particularly the development of techniques and instruments that allowed for its negotiability and the development of discounting methods. Negotiability and discounting in turn depended on the creation of institutions that would permit their use and the development of centers where such events could occur – first fairs, such as the Champagne fairs, then banks, and finally financial houses that could specialize in discounting. These developments were a function not only of specific institutions but also of the scale of economic activity. Increasing volume obviously made such institutional developments possible. In addition to the economies of scale necessary for the development of the bills of exchange, improved enforce-ability of contracts was critical, and the interrelationship between the development of accounting and auditing methods and their use as evidence in the collection of debts and in the enforcement of contracts was important to this improvement (Yamey, 1949; Watts and Zimmerman, 1983).

A third innovation affecting the mobility of capital arose from the problems associated with maintaining control of agents involved in long-distance trade. The traditional resolution of these problems in medieval and early modern times was the use of kinship and family ties to bind agents to principals in ways that provided some assurance to the principal that the orders and directions of the principal were effectively carried out (the church's greater success with agents may have been because of fear of God or belief in a higher purpose). However, as the size and scope of merchant trading empires grew, the extension of discretionary behavior to others than kin of the principal required the development of more elaborate accounting procedures for monitoring the behavior of agents.

The major developments that lowered information costs were the printing of prices of various commodities as well as the printing of manuals that provided information on weights, measures, customs, brokerage fees, postal systems, and, particularly, on the complex exchange rates between monies in Europe and the trading world. Obviously, these developments were primarily a function of the volume of international trade and therefore a consequence of economies of scale.

The final innovation was the transformation of uncertainty into risk. By uncertainty I mean here a condition wherein one cannot ascertain the probability of an event and therefore cannot arrive at a way of insuring against such an occurrence. Risk on the other hand implies the ability to make an actuarial determination of the likelihood of an event and hence insure against such an outcome. We think of insurance and portfolio diversification in the modern world as methods for converting uncertainty into risks and thereby reducing, through the provision of a hedge against variability, the costs of transacting. When we look at the medieval and early modern world, we find precisely the same results. For example, marine insurance evolved from sporadic individual contracts covering partial payments for losses to contracts issued by specialized firms.

By the fifteenth century marine insurance was established on a secure basis. The wording of the policies had already become stereotyped and changed very little during the next three or four hundred years. . . . In the sixteenth century, it was already current practice to use printed forms provided with a few blank spaces for the name of the ship, the name of the master, the amount of the insurance, the premium, and a few other items that were apt to change from one contract to another. (de Roover, 1945, p. 198)

Marine insurance was one example of the development of actuarial, ascertainable risk; another was business organization that spread risk through either portfolio diversification or through institutions that permitted a large number of investors to engage in risky activities. The commenda itself, from its Jewish, Byzantine, and Muslim origins (Udovitch, 1962) through its evolution at the hands of Italians to the English regulated company and finally the joint stock company, provides an evolutionary story of the institutionalization of risk (although as discussed later in this chapter, the developments created new problems of agency for the principals involved).

The specific innovations and particular institutional instruments evolved as a result of the interplay of two fundamental economic forces. One was the economies of scale associated with a growing volume of trade, the other was the development of improved enforcement mechanisms that made possible the enforcement of contracts at lower costs. Surely the causation ran both ways. That is, the increasing volume of long-distance trade raised the rate of return to merchants of devising effective mechanisms for enforcing contracts. In turn, the development of such mechanisms lowered the costs of contracting and made trade more profitable, thereby increasing its volume.

When we look at the development of enforcement mechanisms, we see that the process was a long one. Although a number of courts handled commercial disputes, it is the development and evolution of mechanisms for enforcing agreements by merchants themselves that is of particular interest.[3] Enforceability appears to have had its beginnings in the development of internal codes of conduct in fraternal orders of guild merchants; those who did not live up to them were threatened with ostracism. Merchants carried with them in long-distance trade codes of conduct, so that Pisan laws passed into the sea codes of Marseilles. Oleron and Lubeck gave laws to the north of Europe, Barcelona to the south of Europe, and from Italy came the legal principle of insurance and bills of exchange (Mitchell, 1969, p. 156).

The development of more sophisticated accounting methods and the use of such methods and of notarial records for evidence in disputes permitted evidence to become the basis for ascertaining facts in disputes.

[3]The following brief discussion of the evolution of law has been substantially improved thanks to the critical comments on an earlier draft by John Drobak and William Jones of the Washington University law faculty and Dick Helmholz of the University of Chicago law faculty. I wish to thank them and absolve them from any blame should there be any remaining errors.

The gradual blending of the voluntaristic structure of enforcement of contracts via internal merchant organizations with enforcement by the state is an important part of the story of increasing the enforceability of contracts. The long evolution of merchant law from its voluntary beginnings and the differences in resolutions that it had with both the common and Roman law are a part of the story. The two types of law did not accommodate each other very well to begin with. This was particularly true in cases of moral hazard and asymmetric information in insurance contracts as well as those associated with fraud in exchange. The law merchant codes were assumed by the courts of common law in England, but continued to be administered in the original spirit of the law merchant, that is as a law based on custom. Cases seldom laid down a particular rule because it was virtually impossible to separate custom from the facts. The habit was to leave the jury with the custom and the facts and the judge would charge the jury to determine and apply the custom when supported by the facts. Eventually, this policy was changed. When Lord Mansfield became chief justice of the English court of King's Bench in 1756 he gave force to the existing customs. He established general principles that were to be used to rule future cases. He was not too fond of English common law and as a result he derived many of these principles from the writings of foreign jurists (Scrutton, 1891, p. 15).

The law merchant, besides providing a much needed court of law especially suited to the unique needs of the merchant, also fostered some significant developments that aided in decreasing transactions costs of exchange. Among such developments can be included the recognition of the responsibility of the principal for his agent (built upon the Roman law of mandate). This spawned both a benefit and a cost. It allowed the merchant to expand his scope of operation via a series of agents. At the same time it increased the principal-agent problem. Initially this legal recognition was in effect only for well known agents of the principal. The fact that credit was generally given to the agent because it was generally believed he was acting for his master provided an obvious opportunity for the agent to benefit himself. At the same time, however, the privilege was also used to control the principal-agent problem. By extending to his agent the privilege of using the merchant's credit for his own personal trading, the merchant was able to increase the opportunity cost to the agent of losing his position. If the agent abused his position, he would lose not only his job, but a valuable line of credit as well.

The effect of the merchant law on contracts and sales was especially encouraging to the expansion of trade. The existing Roman and Germanic laws did not give the security and certainty of bargains to merchants that was needed. Neither body of law protected them against the claims of the original owner of stolen or lost goods that the merchant had innocently purchased. The feudal lord recognized the value of fairs and markets as a revenue source and the importance of protecting the honest purchaser. Under merchant law, the honest purchaser was allowed either to keep the goods or to be refunded the purchase price if the goods were returned to the original owner.

Protection of the bona fide purchaser was not a part of the common law. However, in commercial disputes the good faith principle was used earlier and on a much wider scope (the basis of Roman contract law by A.D. 200). It evolved first out of the fair bonds, which validated sales at fairs by affixing a seal to the bond. Originally this was a voluntary measure – the custom of fairs allowed debts to be contracted by witness. Eventually though, the desire to avoid fraud and at the same time increase revenue led to a law requiring that all sales be recognized by a sealed bond. Once sealed, the bond could be invalidated only by proving that the seal had been forged.

Many rules of merchant law developed because common law interfered with trade. For example, the common law's failure to protect bona fide purchasers forced examining the title of goods all the way back to the original owner. This presented an obvious problem for merchants. The cost and time required to carry out such a search were prohibitive and caused the first exception to common law that the law merchant made. The evolution of the situation from the thirteenth to the sixteenth century can be measured by the manner in which purchasers of goods with fraudulent titles were treated. In the thirteenth century, the purchaser of such goods would be forced to return them upon the discovery of a discrepancy anywhere along the chain of ownership of the good. By the time Edmund Coke was appointed chief justice in 1606, the final (good faith) purchaser of a good was recognized (in certain, but not all, courts) as having the only viable title to the good, making any legal purchase he made legal all the way back down the chain of ownership.

A major player in this evolution was the state, and there was continuous interplay between the fiscal needs of the state and its credibility in its relationships with merchants and the citizenry in general. In particular, the evolution of capital markets was critically influenced by the policies of the state, because to the extent that the state was bound by commitments that it would not confiscate assets or in any way use its coercive power to increase uncertainty in exchange, it made possible the evolution of financial institutions and the creation of more efficient capital markets. The shackling of arbitrary behavior of rulers and the development of impersonal rules that successfully bound both the state and voluntary organizations were a key part of this institutional transformation. The development of an institutional process by which government debt could be circulated became a part of a regular capital market, and the process that enabled a government debt to be funded by regular sources of taxation was a major step in the evolution of capital markets (Tracy, 1985; North and Weingast, 1989).

It was in the Netherlands, and Amsterdam specifically, that these diverse innovations and institutions were put together to create the predecessor of the efficient modern set of markets that make possible the growth of exchange and commerce. An open immigration policy attracted businessmen; efficient methods of financing long-distance trade were developed, as were capital markets and discounting methods in financial houses that lowered the costs of underwriting this trade. The development of techniques for spreading risk and transforming uncertainty into actuarial, ascertainable risks, the creation of large-scale markets that allowed for lowering the costs of information, and the development of negotiable government indebtedness all were a part of this story (Barbour, 1950).

V

These stories of stability and change go to the heart of the puzzle about the human economic condition. In the former cases (of primitive exchange) maximizing activity by the actors will not induce increments to knowledge and skills or otherwise modify the institutional framework to induce greater productivity; in the latter case (of Western Europe) the evolution is a consistent story of incremental change induced by the private gains to be realized by productivity raising organizational and institutional changes. To make the story more convincing one needs to link the changes in Western Europe with the overall ways that the stock of knowledge and its applications are evolving and interacting with the economic and political structure. Doing so would entail an examination of the way competition among political units, the disintegration of the intellectual authority of the church, and evolving military technology all interacted with the development and application of knowledge and skills.

A traditional explanation for European success in contrast to China, Islam, or other areas is competition amongst political units. There can be little doubt that this competition is an important part of the story, but clearly it is not the whole story. Parts of Europe failed to develop. Spain and Portugal stagnated for centuries and economic growth in the rest of Europe was uneven at best. It was the Netherlands and England that were carriers of institutional change. The characteristics of path dependence, described in the previous chapters, set within the context of the contrasting *initial* conditions produced the divergent stories of England and Spain.

14

Incorporating institutional analysis into economic history: prospects and puzzles

I

What difference does the explicit incorporation of institutional analysis make to the writing (and for that matter the reading) of economic history and of history in general? Writing history is constructing a coherent story of some facet of the human condition through time. Such a construction exists only in the human mind. We do not recreate the past; we construct stories about the past. But to be good history, the story must give a consistent, logical account and be constrained by the available evidence and the available theory. A brief answer to the question is that incorporating institutions into history allows us to tell a much better story than we otherwise could. The precliometric economic history actually was built around institutions, and in the hands of its most accomplished practitioners it managed to provide us with a picture of continuity and institutional change, that is, with an evolutionary story. But because it was built on bits and pieces of theory and statistics that had no overall structure, it did not lend itself to generalizations or analysis extending beyond the essentially ad hoc character of individual stories. The cliometric contribution was the application of a systematic body of theory – neoclassical theory – to history and the application of sophisticated, quantitative techniques to the specification and testing of historical models.

However, we have paid a big price for the uncritical acceptance of neoclassical theory. Although the systematic application of price theory to economic history was a major contribution, neoclassical theory is concerned with the allocation of resources at a moment of time, a devastatingly limiting feature to historians whose central question is to account for change over time. Moreover, the allocation was assumed to occur in a frictionless world, that is, one in which institutions either did not exist or did not matter. These two conditions gave away what economic history is really all about: to attempt to explain the diverse patterns of growth, stagnation, and decay of societies over time, and to explore the way in which the frictions that are the consequences of human interaction produce widely divergent results.

By applying neoclassical theory to history economic historians were able to focus upon choices and constraints, which were certainly all to the good. That is, we could look at what the constraints were that defined and limited the set of choices of human beings. The constraints, however, were not imposed by the limitations of human organization, but only those of technology and income. And even technology, at least in the neoclassical framework, was always an exogenous factor and thus never really fit into the theory. Although a great deal of important work has been done on the history of technology and its relationship to economic performance, it has essentially remained outside any formal body of theory. The exception was the work of Karl Marx, who attempted to integrate technological change with institutional change. Marx's early elaboration of the productive forces (by which he usually meant the state of technology) with the relations of production (by which he meant aspects of human organization and particularly property rights) was a pioneering effort to integrate the limits and constraints of technology with those of human organization.[1]

But Marx's story had a utopian ending (although the evil forces along the way continue to provide the Marxist writer with villains aplenty), whereas the institutional analysis in this study provides no guarantee of a happy ending.

Precliometric economic historians also placed technology on center stage. Indeed, the story of the Industrial Revolution as the great watershed in human history is built around a discontinuous rate of technological change occurring in the eighteenth century. That makes technology the creator of human well-being and posits utopia to be a simple story of increasing productive capacity.

Marxist theory is deficient because it entails a fundamental change in human behavior to achieve its results, and we have no evidence of such a change (even after seventy years of socialist society).[2] The traditional

---

[1]See North, "Is It Worth Making Sense of Marx?" (1986) in the symposium on Jon Elster's *Making Sense of Marx* and N. Rosenberg, "Karl Marx and the Economic Role of Science" (1974).

[2]However, it should be noted that ideology plays a big part in the institutional model in this book, and ideology does change people's behavior. But the most striking piece of evidence about ideology with respect to socialist and utopian societies is that however powerful it may be as an initiating force in overcoming the free-rider problem and creating revolutionary cadres or otherwise inducing people to behave differently, it tends to fade over time when it runs counter to the behavioral sources of individual wealth maximizing, as recent events in Eastern Europe attest.

historian's focus on the Industrial Revolution and technological change as the key to utopia is likewise deficient because much of the world has failed to realize the potential benefits of technology. Indeed modern technology may exacerbate many of the problems of human conflict. Certainly the technology has made the conflict more deadly.

There is a different, and I think, better story. It concerns the endless struggle of human beings to solve the problems of cooperation so that they may reap the advantages not only of technology, but also of all the other facets of human endeavor that constitute civilization.

II

The emphasis on technology made a salutory contribution to the writing of economic history. A number of post-World War II studies by Simon Kuznets, Robert Solow, Edward Dennison, Moses Abramovitz, and John Kendrick led to the exploration of the sources of economic growth in terms of analyzing productivity change. Although four decades of study have still not unraveled all the mysteries of the sources of productivity change, they have increased our knowledge about the basic underlying forces of economic growth, and focusing on productivity growth is undoubtedly the right direction to go in exploring those underlying determinants. Technology provided an upper bound to realizable economic growth. To put it simply in the context of this book, in a zero transaction cost world, increases in the stock of knowledge and its application (both physical and human capital) provide a key to the potential well-being of human beings in societies. What was left out of the analysis was why the potential was not realized, and why there is such an enormous gap between the rich countries and the poor countries when the technology is, for the most part, available to everyone. The gap in the real world is paralleled by the gap in the theories and model building of economists.

Neoclassical theory does not directly deal with the issues of growth itself. Nevertheless, in terms of the theory's basic postulates, it is reasonable to assume that the problem of growth is not a real one (although rates of growth might vary). Because output is determined by the stock of capital, both physical and human, and we can increase the stock of capital in the neoclassical world by investing at whatever margins have the highest rate of return, there is no fixed factor. We can overcome resource scarcities by investing in new technologies and we can overcome any other scarcity by investing in new knowledge to overcome that potentially fixed factor. But surely this neoclassical formulation has, as noted above, begged all the interesting questions. To put the issue starkly, recent neoclassical models of growth built around increasing returns (Romer, 1986) and physical and human capital accumulation (Lucas, 1988) crucially depend upon the existence of an implicit incentive structure that drives the models. Baumol's study (1986) implicitly arrives at this conclusion when he finds convergence only among sixteen advanced economies (ones with roughly similar incentive structures), but not with centrally planned economies nor with less-developed countries (with clearly different incentive structures). To attempt to account for the diverse historical experience of economies or the current differential performance of advanced, centrally planned economies and less-developed economies without making the incentive structure derived from institutions an essential ingredient appears to me to be a sterile exercise.

At the other extreme are Marxist models or analytical frameworks initially inspired by Marxist models that do crucially depend on institutional considerations. Whether they are theories of imperialism, dependency, or core/periphery they have in common institutional constructs that result in exploitation and/or uneven patterns of growth and income distribution. To the extent that these models convincingly relate institutions to incentives to choices to outcomes they are consistent with the argument of this study. And because much of human economic history is a story of humans with unequal bargaining strength maximizing their own well-being, it would be amazing if such maximizing activity were not frequently at the expense of others. Indeed, a central theme of this study is the problem of achieving cooperative solutions to problems. More common have been exchange structures that reflected unequal access to resources, capital, and information and hence produced very uneven results for the players. However, to the extent that exploitation models are to be convincing, they must demonstrate that the institutional framework does indeed produce the systematic uneven consequences implied by the theory.

Both the neoclassical and *exploitation* models are driven by wealth-maximizing players and hence shaped by the institutional incentive structure. The difference is that the implicit institutional structure in the former produces efficient competitive markets and the economy, driven by increasing returns or capital accumulation, grows. In the latter, growth of the imperialist or core economy occurs as a result of an institutional structure that exploits the dependent or periphery economies. Because both historical and current economies contain examples of growing economies and stagnant or declining economies, it would be valuable to sort out just what institutional characteristics have shaped performance. What makes for efficient markets? If poor countries are poor because they are the victims of an institutional structure that prevents growth, is that institutional structure imposed from without or is it endogenously determined or is it some combination of both? The systematic study of institutions should answer these questions. Specifically, we must develop empirical data on transaction and transformation costs in such economies and then trace the institutional origins of such costs. In Chapter 8, I provided a very brief examination of the transaction costs and the underlying institutions in the U.S. residential housing market. That chapter also made brief reference to the high cost of transacting and transforming in Third World economies; but idiosyncratic illustrations, such as the length of time in getting spare parts or a telephone, are only illustrative. Still to be undertaken is systematic empirical work that will identify the costs and underlying institutions that make economies unproductive. Then we will be in the position to ascertain the sources of those institutions.

III

I would like to have this concluding chapter demonstrate that the questions raised in this and earlier chapters have been answered. They have not, but I do believe that the analytical framework has answered some and offers the promise of answering still unresolved ones. Let us see where we are.

Incentives are the underlying determinants of economic performance. They are implicit in the theories we have employed and assumed to have a particular form and effect. Bringing incentives up front focuses attention where it belongs, on the key to the performance of economies. The central argument advanced in the foregoing chapters is that incentives have varied immensely over time and still do. Integrating institutional analysis into economics and economic history is redirecting emphasis, but not abandoning the theoretical tools already developed. Redirecting the emphasis entails modifying the notion and implications of rationality, incorporating ideas and ideologies into our analysis, explicitly studying the costs of transacting for the functioning of political and economic markets, and understanding the consequences of path dependence for the historical evolution of economies. At the same time, the underlying tools of neoclassical price theory and the sophisticated quantitative techniques developed by a generation of cliometricians continue to be a part of the tool kit. How does such an approach alter our perception and writing of economic history? Let me illustrate from U.S. economic history.

Institutional analysis brings into the theoretical framework the critical importance of the English heritage of institutions and ideas for the creation of the colonial economy and the relatively efficient markets that characterized that era. The organizations that arose to take advantage of the resultant opportunities – plantations, merchants, shipping firms, family farms – produced a thriving colonial economy. The heritage was not just economic but political and intellectual as well – town meetings and self-government, colonial assemblies, and the intellectual traditions from Hobbes and Locke are essential to integrate the events of 1763 to 1789 into a story of political and economic organizations driven by their subjective perception of the issues that produced the institutional structure of the newly independent nation. Although we have always understood the importance of the political and intellectual currents, an institutional framework can shift the analysis from ad hoc descriptions to an integrated story and will, in consequence, achieve a much deeper understanding of this critical period in U.S. history.

The nineteenth-century U.S. economy provided a hospitable environment for economic growth. Just what made the environment hospitable has certainly occupied the attention of scholars examining the consequences of the Constitution, the evolution of the law, the role of the frontier, the attitude of both the native born and immigrants, and a number of other characteristics of the society that influenced incentives. In fact, it was the adaptively efficient characteristics of the institutional matrix (both the formal rules and the informal constraints embodied in attitudes and values) that produced an economic and political environment that rewarded productive activity of organizations and their development of skills and knowledge. Exactly what was essential to that matrix, what was deliberately created to encourage productivity growth and flexible responses, and what was an accidental by-product of other objectives constitutes an important agenda for a much deeper understanding of economic growth.

We have also paid a good deal of attention to the costs entailed in that growth. Part of those costs was the price paid for adaptive efficiency. The system wiped out losers and there were lots of them – farmers that went bust on the frontier, shipping firms that failed as we lost our comparative advantage in shipping, laborers that suffered unemployment and declining wages from immigrant competition in the 1850s. Part of the costs, however, was a consequence of institutions that exploited individuals and groups – Indians, slaves, and not infrequently immigrants, workers, and farmers to the benefit of those with superior bargaining power. In short, both the sources of growth and the costs entailed in that growth are a common derivative of that institutional framework.

The political framework resulted in the losers having, albeit imperfect, access to remedies for their perceived sources of misfortune. Perceived sources consisted of immediately observed grievances filtered through ongoing intellectual currents and ideologies of the actors. The farmer could frequently observe price discrimination by the railroad or the grain elevator, but the Populist Party platform reflected overall ideological views such as the perceived burden of the gold standard, widespread monopoly, and the pernicious consequences of bankers. We cannot make sense out of the protest movements and policy prescriptions of the period without understanding those intellectual currents.

Nor can we make sense out of the direction of change in the polity and the economy that resulted from those movements without an understanding of them. Whatever the real underlying sources of the farmers' plight that produced discontent in the late nineteenth century, it was the farmers' perceptions that mattered and resulted in changing the political and economic institutional framework.

But it was not just the farmers' perceptions that mattered. It was also the evolving subjective models of the actors of other organizations able to influence outcomes as a consequence of the institutional matrix. Whether the Supreme Court understood the implications of *Munn* v. *Illinois* and the many other Court decisions that gradually altered the legal framework depended on whether the information feedback on the consequences of existing laws was accurate and hence gave them true models. True or false, the models they acted upon were incrementally altering the judicial framework.

An overall contribution that institutional analysis can make to U.S. economic history is to make it a truly historical story, something that has been lost with cliometrics. Much of that history is path dependent simply by nature of constraints from the past imposing limits on current choices and therefore making the current choice set intelligible. But much of it reflects a more fundamental role of path dependence as a consequence of the increasing returns characteristics of the institutional matrix. The reinforcing role that the political and economic organizations provided the institutional matrix via network externalities and the other sources of increasing returns provided the decisive stamp to U.S. economic history. But the organizations were also inducing incremental change and that blend of underlying stability and incremental change can give us a deeper and more satisfying account of that history.

IV

I conclude this study by speculating about the central issue of economic history. Institutions determine the performance of economies, but what creates *efficient* institutions? Clearly the existence of relatively productive institutions somewhere in the world and low-cost information about the resultant performance characteristics of those institutions is a powerful incentive to change for poorly performing economies. That appears to be the case in the striking changes in Eastern European societies in 1989.

But can we generalize about the forces that will make for such changes? How does one reverse the increasing returns characteristics of a particular institutional matrix? The foregoing analysis provides lots of clues and points, I believe, to two related features of the institutional matrix of economies: the informal constraints and the transaction costs inherent in the political process.

Informal constraints come from the cultural transmission of values, from the extension and application of formal rules to solve specific exchange problems, from the solution to straightforward coordination problems. In total, they appear to have a pervasive influence on the institutional structure. Effective traditions of hard work, honesty, and integrity simply lower the cost of transacting and make possible complex, productive exchange. Such traditions are always reinforced by ideologies that undergird those attitudes. Where do these attitudes and ideologies come from and how do they change? The subjective perceptions of the actors are not just culturally derived but are continually being modified by experience that is filtered through existing (culturally determined) mental constructs. Therefore, fundamental changes in relative prices will gradually alter norms and ideologies, and the lower the costs of information, the more rapid the alterations.

A major theme of Chapter 12 has been that the cost of transacting in even the most perfect of political markets is relatively high. The result is that the political actor frequently has substantial degrees of freedom in making choices. Whatever the outcome of the principal/agent controversy with respect to the freedom of members of Congress from constituent constraints in the modern U.S. political scene (Kalt and Zupan, 1984), the political actor throughout history and in the Third World and Eastern European polities has been far less constrained by *constituent* interests. Under certain circumstances, the politician will bear the costs of organizing and/or provide a legal framework in which binding commitments can be enforced. That may encourage the formation of groups that may institute more radical economic change. The key is the incentives facing the politician that make some of the constituents – those willing to undertake change – more important than others. The political actor, then, is in the position of being able to initiate more radical change.[3]

We can tie these two features together by returning again to a discussion of seventeenth-century English political change. In a recent essay with Barry Weingast (North and Weingast, 1989) we maintained that the fundamental changes in the English polity as a consequence of the Glorious Revolution were a critical contributing factor to the development of the English economy. The outline of events is as follows. In the

[3]Robert Bates's recent study (1989) of the political economy of Kenya since the Mau-Mau revolt and independence provides interesting empirical content to this argument, and I am indebted to him for forcefully reminding me of this aspect of his study.

early seventeenth century, repeated fiscal crises of the Stuarts led them to engage in forced loans, to sell monopolies, and to engage in a variety of practices (including wealth confiscation) that rendered property rights less secure. Both Parliament and the common law courts became engaged in an ongoing struggle with the Crown. This led, ultimately, to civil war, followed by several failed experiments with alternative political institutions. The monarchy was restored in 1660, but the result was a repetition of the political struggle over Stuart fiscal prerogatives and ultimately the king was deposed. The revolutionaries had sought to solve the problem of controlling the Crown's exercise of arbitrary and confiscatory power.[4] Parliamentary supremacy, central (parliamentary) control in financial matters, curtailment of royal prerogative powers, independence of the judiciary (at least from the Crown), and the supremacy of the common law courts were established. A major consequence was an increased security of property rights.

The most striking immediate consequence was the rapid development of the capital market. Following the Glorious Revolution, not only did the government become financially solvent but it gained access to an unprecedented level of funds. In just nine years (from 1688 to 1697) government borrowing increased by an order of magnitude. The sharp change in the willingness of lenders to supply funds reflected a clear perception that the government would honor its agreements.

The formation of the Bank of England in 1694 for intermediating public debt also led it to undertake private operations. Numerous other banks also began operation at this time. A wide range of securities and negotiable instruments emerged in the early eighteenth century and interest rates on private credit appear to have roughly paralleled rates on public credit.

The security of property rights and the development of the public and private capital market were instrumental factors not only in England's subsequent rapid economic development, but in its political hegemony and ultimate dominance of the world. England could not have beaten France without its financial revolution (Dickson, 1967); the funds made available by the growth in debt from 1688 to 1697 were a necessary condition for England's success in the ongoing war with France as well as in the next one (from 1703 to 1714) from which England emerged the major power in the world.

Do we attribute the rise of England to the political struggle and eventual triumph of Parliament? Certainly that was the proximate source and

[4]Such a characterization sounds suspiciously like Whig history, but in fact is only meant to reflect their perception of the issues. There is no implication that the motives of the revolutionaries were any purer than those of the Crown or even that they had some superior vision of societal evolution.

a necessary condition for English success. It is tempting to claim too much. Would England really have followed the path of Continental countries if the Stuarts had won? One could tell a plausible counterfactual that put more weight on the fundamental strength of English property rights and the common law that would have ultimately circumscribed royal behavior. Recall the discussion in Chapter 12 on path dependence, in which English social attitudes and norms appear to have been strikingly different from those of the Continent. What role did the informal constraints play in setting the scene for the events of the seventeenth century? To what extent were the subjective perceptions of the political actors that led them to make the choices that resulted in revolution a function of the informal constraints and accompanying ideology? We do not have neat and definite answers to these questions. But it appears plausible that the underlying informal constraints were hospitable to the change in the formal rules. The best evidence to support the contention is the stability of the consequent political-economic system. When there is a radical change in the formal rules that makes them inconsistent with the existing informal constraints, there is an unresolved tension between them that will lead to long-run political instability.

One gets *efficient* institutions by a polity that has built-in incentives to create and enforce efficient property rights. But it is hard — maybe impossible — to model such a polity with wealth-maximizing actors unconstrained by other considerations. It is no accident that economic models of the polity developed in the public choice literature make the state into something like the Mafia — or, to employ its terminology, a leviathan. The state then becomes nothing more than a machine to redistribute wealth and income. Now we do not have to look far afield to observe states with such characteristics. But the traditional public choice literature is clearly not the whole story, as this study has attempted to demonstrate. Informal constraints matter. We need to know much more about culturally derived norms of behavior and how they interact with formal rules to get better answers to such issues. We are just beginning the serious study of institutions. The promise is there. We may never have definitive answers to all our questions. But we can do better.

References

Akerlof, George A. 1970. "The Market for 'Lemons': Qualitative Uncertainty and the Market Mechanism." *Quarterly Journal of Economics*, 84:488–500.

Alchian, Armen A. 1950. "Uncertainty, Evolution and Economic Theory." *Journal of Political Economy*, 58:211–21.

Arthur, W. Brian. 1988. "Self-Reinforcing Mechanisms in Economics." In Philip W. Anderson, Kenneth J. Arrow, and David Pines (eds.), *The Economy as an Evolving Complex System*. Reading, MA.: Addison-Wesley.

. 1989. "Competing Technologies, Increasing Returns, and Lock-In by Historical Events." *Economic Journal*, 99:116–31.

Axelrod, Robert. 1984. *The Evolution of Cooperation*. New York: Basic Books.

. 1986. "An Evolutionary Approach to Norms." *American Political Science Review*, 80:1095–111.

Barbour, Violet. 1950. *Capitalism in Amsterdam in the Seventeenth Century*. Baltimore: Johns Hopkins University Press.

Barzel, Yoram. 1977. "An Economic Analysis of Slavery." *Journal of Law and Economics*, 20:87–110.

. 1982. "Measurement Cost and the Organization of Markets." *Journal of Law and Economics*, 25:27–48.

. 1989. *Economic Analysis of Property Rights*. Cambridge: Cambridge University Press.

Bates, Robert H. 1987. *Essays on the Political Economy of Rural Africa*. Berkeley: University of California Press.

. 1989. *Beyond the Miracle of the Market: The Political Economy of Agrarian Development in Rural Kenya*. Cambridge: Cambridge University Press.

Baumol, William J. 1986. "Productivity Growth, Convergence, and Welfare: What the Long Run Data Show." *American Economic Review*, 76:1072–85.

Becker, Gary S. 1965. "A Theory of the Allocation of Time." *Economic Journal*, 75:493–517.

. 1981. *A Treatise on the Family*. Cambridge, MA.: Harvard University Press.

. 1983. "A Theory of Competition Among Pressure Groups." *Quarterly Journal of Economics*, 98:372–99.

and George Stigler. 1977. "De Gustibus Non Est Disputandum." *American Economic Review*, 67:76–90.

References

Boyd, R. and P. J. Richerson. 1985. *Culture and the Evolutionary Process*. Chicago: University of Chicago Press.

Buchanan, James M. and Gordon Tullock. 1962. *The Calculus of Consent*. Ann Arbor: University of Michigan Press.

Carstensen, V. (ed.). 1963. *The Public Lands*. Madison: University of Wisconsin Press.

Cavalli-Sforza, L. L. and M. W. Feldman. 1981. *Cultural Transmission and Evolution: A Quantitative Approach*. Princeton: Princeton University Press.

Chandler, Alfred. 1977. *The Visible Hand*. Cambridge, MA.: Harvard University Press.

Cheung, Steven N. S. 1974. "A Theory of Price Control." *Journal of Law and Economics*, 12:23–45.

. 1983. "The Contractual Nature of the Firm." *Journal of Law and Economics*, 17:53–71.

Coase, Ronald H. 1937. "The Nature of the Firm." *Economica*, 4:386–405.

. 1960. "The Problem of Social Cost." *Journal of Law and Economics*, 3:1–44.

Coatsworth, John H. 1978. "Obstacles to Economic Growth in Nineteenth-Century Mexico." *American Historical Review*, 83:80–100.

Colson, Elizabeth. 1974. *Tradition and Contract: The Problem of Order*. Chicago: Adeline.

David, Paul. 1975. *Technical Choice, Innovation and Economic Growth*. Cambridge: Cambridge University Press.

. 1985. "Clio and the Economics of QWERTY." *American Economic Review*, 75:332–37.

Dawkins, R. 1976. *The Selfish Gene*. Oxford: Oxford University Press.

Demsetz, Harold. 1988. "The Theory of the Firm Revisited." *Journal of Law, Economics and Organization*, 4:141–62.

de Roover, Florence E. 1945. "Early Examples of Marine Insurance." *Journal of Economic History*, 5:172–200.

de Soto, Hernando. 1989. *The Other Path: The Invisible Revolution in the Third World*. New York: Harper & Row.

De Vries, Jan. 1976. *The Economy in Europe in an Age of Crisis, 1600–1750*. Cambridge: Cambridge University Press.

Dickson, Peter G. M. 1967. *The Financial Revolution in England: A Study in the Development of Public Credit, 1688–1756*. London: St. Martin's.

Eggertsson, Thrainn. 1990. *Economic Behavior and Institutions*. Cambridge: Cambridge University Press.

Ellickson, Robert. 1986. "Of Coase and Cattle: Dispute Resolution Among Neighbors in Shasta County." *Stanford Law Review*, 38:624–87.

. 1987. "A Critique of Economic and Sociological Theories of Social Control." *Journal of Legal Studies*, 16:67–100.

Ellickson, Robert. Forthcoming. *Order without Law*. Cambridge, Mass.: Harvard University Press.

Evans-Pritchard, E. 1940. *The Nuer*. Oxford: Oxford University Press.

Fogel, Robert. 1989. *Without Consent or Contract*. New York: Norton.

Frank, Robert H. 1987. "If Homo Economicus Could Choose His Own Utility Function Would He Want One with a Conscience." *American Economic Review*, 77:593–604.

. 1988. *Passions Within Reason: The Strategic Role of Emotions*. New York: Norton.

Fuchs, Victor. 1983. *How We Live: An Economic Perspective From Birth to Death*. Cambridge: Harvard University Press.

References

Geertz, Clifford. 1979. *"Suq: The Bazaar Economy in Sefrou."* In C. Geertz, H. Geertz and L. Rosen, *Meaning and Order in Moroccan Society.* Cambridge University Press.

Geertz, C., H. Geertz, and L. Rosen. 1979. *Meaning and Order in Moroccan Society.* Cambridge: Cambridge University Press.

Glade, William P. 1969. *The Latin American Economies: A Study of Their Institutional Evolution.* New York: American Book.

Goldberg, Victor. 1976. *"Regulation and Administered Contracts."* *Bell Journal of Economics,* 7:426–8.

Hahn, F. H. 1987. *"Information, Dynamics and Equilibrium."* *Scottish Journal of Political Economy,* 34:321–34.

Hardin, Russell. 1982. *Collective Action.* Baltimore: Johns Hopkins University Press.

Hargreaves-Heap, Shaun. 1989. *Rationality in Economics.* New York: Blackwell.

Hashimoto, Masanori. 1979. *"Bonus-Payments, On-The-Job Training and Lifetime Employment in Japan."* *Journal of Political Economy,* 87:1086–104.

Hayek, F. A. 1960. *The Constitution of Liberty.* Chicago: University of Chicago Press.

Heiner, Ronald. 1983. *"The Origins of Predictable Behavior."* *American Economic Review,* 73:560–95.

. 1986. *"Imperfect Decisions and the Law: On the Evolution of Legal Precedent and Rules."* *Journal of Legal Studies,* 15:227–62.

Herrnstein, Richard. 1988. *"A Behavioral Alternative to Utility Maximization."* In S. Maital (ed.), *Applied Behavioral Economics,* Volume 1. New York: New York University Press.

Hirshleifer, Jack. 1987. *Economic Behavior in Adversity.* Chicago: University of Chicago Press.

Hoffman, Elizabeth and Matthew L. Spitzer. 1985. *"Entitlements, Rights and Fairness: Some Experimental Results."* *Journal of Legal Studies,* 14:259–98.

Hogarth, R., and M. Reder (eds.). 1986. *The Behavioral Foundations of Economic Theory. Journal of Business* (supplement).

Holmstrom, Bengt. 1979. *"Moral Hazard and Observability."* *Bell Journal of Economics,* 10:74–91.

Hughes, J. R. T. 1987. *"The Great Land Ordinances."* In D. Klingaman and R. Vedder (eds.), *Essays on the Old Northwest.* Athens: Ohio University Press.

Jensen, M. and W. Meckling. 1976. *"Theory of the Firm: Managerial Behavior, Agency Costs, and Capital Structure."* *Journal of Financial Economics,* 3:305–360.

Johansson, S. Ryan. 1988. *"The Computer Paradigm and the Role of Cultural Information in Social Systems."* *Historical Methods,* 21:172–88.

Kahneman, D., J. L. Knetsch and R. H. Thaler. 1986. *"Fairness and the Assumptions of Economics."* In Robin M. Hogarth and Melvin W. Reder (eds.), *The Behavioral Foundations of Economic Theory. Journal of Business* (supplement), 59:S285–S300.

Kalt, Joseph P. and Mark A. Zupan. 1984. *"Capture and Ideology in the Economic Theory of Politics."* *American Economic Review,* 74:279–300.

Klein, Benjamin and Keith Leffler. 1981. *"The Role of Market Forces in Assuring Contractual Performance."* *Journal of Political Economy,* 89:615–41.

Knight, Frank H. 1921. *Risk, Uncertainty and Profit.* Boston: Houghton Mifflin.

Kreps, David. Forthcoming. *"Corporate Culture and Economic Theory."* In James Alt and Kenneth Shepsle (eds.), *Perspectives on Positive Political Economy.* Cambridge: Cambridge University Press.

References

Lancaster, K. 1966. "A New Approach to Consumer Theory." *Journal of Political Economy,* 74:132–57.

Libecap, Gary D. 1989. *Contracting for Property Rights.* Cambridge: Cambridge University Press.

    and Steven N. Wiggins. 1985. "The Influence of Private Contractual Failure on Regulation: The Case of Oil Field Unitization." *Journal of Political Economy,* 93:690–714.

Lopez, Robert S. and Irving W. Raymond. 1955. *Medieval Trade in the Mediterranean.* New York: Columbia University Press.

Lucas, Robert E., Jr. 1986. "Adaptive Behavior and Economic Theory." In Robin M. Hogarth and Melvin W. Reder (eds.), *The Behavioral Foundations of Economic Theory. Journal of Business* (supplement), 59:S401–S26.

    . 1988. "On the Mechanics of Economic Development." *Journal of Monetary Economics,* 22:3–42.

Macfarlane, Alan. 1978. *The Origins of English Individualism: The Family, Property, and Social Transition.* Oxford: Blackwell.

Machina, Mark. 1987. "Choice Under Uncertainty: Problems Solved and Unsolved." *Journal of Economic Perspectives,* 1:121–54.

Marglin, Stephen. 1974. "What Do Bosses Do?" *Review of Radical Political Economy,* 6:33–60.

Margolis, Howard. 1982. *Selfishness, Altruism and Rationality: A Theory of Social Choice.* Cambridge: Cambridge University Press.

Milgrom, Paul R., Douglass C. North, and Barry W. Weingast. 1990. "The Role of Institutions in the Revival of Trade: The Law Merchant, Private Judges, and the Champagne Fairs." *Economics and Politics,* 2:1–23.

Miller, Gary. Forthcoming. *Managerial Dilemmas: The Political Economy of Hierarchies.* Cambridge: Cambridge University Press.

Mitchell, William. 1969. *An Essay on the Early History of the Law Merchant.* New York: Burt Franklin Press.

Nelson, Douglas and Eugene Silberberg. 1987. "Ideology and Legislator Shirking." *Economic Inquiry,* 25:15–25.

Nelson, Richard. Forthcoming. "Capitalism as an Engine of Progress." *Research Policy.*

    and Sidney G. Winter. 1982. *An Evolutionary Theory of Economic Change.* Cambridge: Harvard University Press.

North, Douglass C. 1955. "Location Theory and Regional Economic Growth." *Journal of Political Economy,* 63:243–58.

    . 1981. *Structure and Change in Economic History.* New York: Norton.

    . 1984. "Government and the Cost of Exchange." *Journal of Economic History,* 44:255–64.

    . 1986. "Is It Worth Making Sense of Marx?" *Inquiry,* 29:57–64.

    . Forthcoming. "Institutions, Transaction Costs, and the Rise of Merchant Empires." In James D. Tracy (ed.), *The Political Economy of Merchant Empires.* Cambridge: Cambridge University Press.

    and Andrew Rutten. 1987. "The Northwest Ordinance in Historical Perspective." In D. Klingaman and R. Vedder (eds.), *Essays on the Old Northwest.* Athens: Ohio University Press.

    and Robert P. Thomas. 1973. *The Rise of the Western World: A New Economic History.* Cambridge: Cambridge University Press.

    and Barry W. Weingast. 1989. "The Evolution of Institutions Governing Public Choice in 17th Century England." *Journal of Economic History,* 49:803–32.

References

Olson, Mancur. 1965. *The Logic of Collective Action*. Cambridge: Cambridge University Press.

Ostrom, Elinor. 1986. "An Agenda for the Study of Institutions." *Public Choice,* 48:3–25.

Ostrom, Vincent. 1971. *The Political Theory of a Compound Republic: A Reconstruction of the Logical Foundations of Democracy as Presented in the Federalist*. Blacksburg, VA.: VPI, Center for Study of Public Choice.

Pelikan, Pavel. 1987. "The Formation of Incentive Mechanisms in Different Economic Systems." In Stefan Hedlund (ed.), *Incentives and Economic Systems*. New York: New York University Press.

Plott, Charles R. 1986. "Rational Choice in Experimental Markets." In Robin M. Hogarth and Melvin W. Reder (eds.), *The Behavioral Foundations of Economic Theory. Journal of Business* (supplement), 59:S301–S28.

Polanyi, M. 1967. *The Tacit Dimension*. Garden City: Doubleday-Anchor.

Posner, Richard A. 1980. "A Theory of Primitive Society, with Special Reference to Law." *Journal of Law and Economics*, 23:1–53.

Riker, William H. 1976. "Comments on Vincent Ostrom's Paper." *Public Choice*, 27:13–15.

Romer, Paul M. 1986. "Increasing Returns and Long-Run Growth." *Journal of Political Economy*, 94:1002–38.

Rosenberg, Nathan. 1972. *Technology and American Economic Growth*. New York: Harper & Row.

. 1974. "Karl Marx on the Economic Role of Science." *Journal of Political Economy*, 82:713–28.

. 1976. *Perspectives on Technology*. Cambridge: Cambridge University Press.

Schmookler, J. 1957. "Inventors Past and Present." *Review of Economics and Statistics*, 39:321–33.

Schofield, Norman. 1985. "Anarchy, Altruism and Cooperation: A Review." *Social Choice and Welfare*, 2:207–19.

Schumpeter, Joseph A. 1934. *The Theory of Economic Development: An Inquiry into Profits, Capital, Interest and the Business Cycle*. Cambridge: Harvard University Press.

. 1954. "The Crisis of the Tax State." *International Economic Papers*, 4:5–38.

Scrutton, Thomas Edward. 1891. *The Elements of Mercantile Law*. London: W. Clowes.

Sheehan, S. 1973. "Peas." *The New Yorker*, 49:103–18.

Shepard, Andrea. 1987. "Licensing to Enhance Demand for New Technologies." *Rand Journal of Economics*, 18:360–68.

Shepsle, Kenneth A. 1986. "Institutional Equilibrium and Equilibrium Institutions." In Herbert Weisberg (ed.) *Political Science: The Science of Politics*. New York: Agathon Press.

. 1989. "The Changing Textbook Congress." In John E. Chubb and Paul E. Peterson (eds.), *Can the Government Govern?* Washington, D.C.: Brookings Institution.

and Barry W. Weingast. 1987. "The Institutional Foundations of Committee Power." *American Political Science Review*, 81:85–104.

Simon, Herbert. 1986. "Rationality in Psychology and Economics." In Robin M. Hogarth and Melvin W. Reder (eds.), *The Behavioral Foundations of Economic Theory. Journal of Business* (supplement), 59:S209–S24.

Skocpol, Theda. 1979. *States and Social Revolutions: A Comparative Analysis of France, Russia and China*. Cambridge: Cambridge University Press.

References

Sokoloff, Kenneth L. 1988. "Inventive Activity in Early Industrial America: Evidence From Patent Records, 1790–1846." *Journal of Economic History,* 58:813–50.

Stubbs, William. 1896. *The Constitutional History of England,* Volume II. Oxford: Clarendon Press.

Sugden, Robert. 1986. *The Economics of Rights, Co-operation, and Welfare.* Oxford: Blackwell.

Taylor, Michael. 1982. *Community, Anarchy and Liberty.* Cambridge: Cambridge University Press.

——. 1987. *The Possibility of Cooperation.* Cambridge: Cambridge University Press.

Tracy, James D. 1985. *A Financial Revolution in the Hapsburg Netherlands: Renten and Renteniers in the County of Holland.* Berkeley: University of California Press.

Udovitch, Abraham. 1962. "At the Origins of the Western *Commenda:* Islam, Israel, Byzantium?" *Speculum,* 37:198–207.

Veitch, John. 1986. "Repudiations and Confiscations by the Medieval State." *Journal of Economic History,* 56:31–6.

Veliz, Claudio. 1980. *The Centralist Tradition in Latin America.* Princeton: Princeton University Press.

Wallis, John J. and Douglass C. North. 1986. "Measuring the Transaction Sector in the American Economy, 1870–1970. In S. L. Engerman and R. E. Gallman (eds.), *Long-Term Factors in American Economic Growth.* Chicago: University of Chicago Press.

Watts, R. L. and J. L. Zimmerman. 1983. "Agency Problems, Auditing and the Theory of the Firm: Some Evidence." *Journal of Law and Economics,* 26:613–33.

Weingast, Barry W. and William Marshall. 1988. "The Industrial Organization of Congress; or, Why Legislatures, Like Firms, Are Not Organized as Markets." *Journal of Political Economy,* 96:132–163.

Williamson, Oliver E. 1975. *Markets and Hierarchies: Analysis and Antitrust Implications.* New York: Free Press.

——. 1985. *The Economic Institutions of Capitalism.* New York: Free Press.

Winter, Sidney G. 1986. "Comments on Arrow and on Lucas." In Robin M. Hogarth and Melvin W. Reder (eds.), *The Behavioral Foundations of Economic Theory. Journal of Business* (supplement), 59:S427–34.

Yamey, B. S. 1949. "Scientific Bookkeeping and the Rise of Capitalism." *Economic History Review,* Second Series, 1:99–113.

Index

Index

Index